William Richard Morfill

Russia

William Richard Morfill

Russia

ISBN/EAN: 9783337298692

Printed in Europe, USA, Canada, Australia, Japan

Cover: Foto ©ninafisch / pixelio.de

More available books at **www.hansebooks.com**

BY

W. R. MORFILL.

Горе тому, у кого языкъ лепечетъ
А голова не вѣдаетъ.
Russian Proverb.

(Woe to him whose tongue chatters, but his head knows nothing.)

WITH ILLUSTRATIONS.

London:
SAMPSON LOW, MARSTON, SEARLE, & RIVINGTON,
CROWN BUILDINGS, 188, FLEET STREET.
1880.

PREFACE.

A FEW words may be necessary as preface to this little work. My object has been to give, in a small compass, an account of the present condition of the Russian Empire, based upon original authorities. I have endeavoured to judge the country fairly, and not merely from an English point of view. I have attempted a genial, perhaps even a sympathetic sketch, and hope not to have failed utterly. To avoid mistakes, I will add that I have freely made use of my own occasional contributions to English periodical literature. It was necessary to say thus much to avoid charges of plagiarism. I hope what Montaigne declared of his book may be true of mine, "C'est un livre de bonne foy, lecteur."

W. R. MORFILL.

OXFORD.

CONTENTS.

CHAPTER I.
Physical Geography of Russia 1

CHAPTER II.
Ethnology 30

CHAPTER III.
Language, Literature, and Art 40

CHAPTER IV.
Chief Cities and their Characteristics . . . 86

CHAPTER V.
Government, Political Life, Church, &c. 121

CHAPTER VI.
Agriculture and Commerce, Resources and Industries. 141

CHAPTER VII.
Social Life and National Characteristics . . 148

CHAPTER VIII.
A Short Sketch of Russian History . . . 172

CHAPTER IX.

Polish History 192

CHAPTER X.

Polish Literature 201

Appendix A. 216
Appendix B. 222
Index 225

LIST OF ILLUSTRATIONS.

Cross at the entrance of a Lithuanian Village . .	12
Kalmuck Village	35
A Lesghian	37
Monastery of Troitza	100
Peasant of the neighbourhood of Riga . . .	112
Irkutsk, on side of the Angara . .	116
Russian Merchant	144
Russian Women	157
A Dealer in Ice	160

RUSSIA.

CHAPTER I.

PHYSICAL GEOGRAPHY OF RUSSIA.

THE vast Empire of Russia which covers so great an extent of Eastern Europe and Northern Asia, extends from the Baltic Sea and the Niemen to Behring Strait and the Pacific. Its most southerly point (about 39° N. lat.) is in Trans-Caucasia, and its most northerly in Siberia (N. E. Cape 77° 20′ N. lat.), thus stretching through nearly 40 degrees of latitude; or, if we wish to map out more minutely its limits, we may say that it has on the N. the Frozen Ocean, on the E. Behring Strait and the Pacific Ocean, on the S. the Chinese Empire, the territories of the independent hordes of the Kirghiz, the steppes of Touran, the Caspian Sea, Persia, Asiatic Turkey, and European

Turkey; on the W., Moldavia, Austria, Prussia, the Baltic Sea, and Sweden.

M. Réclus calculates that Russia is ten times the size of France, and its possessions in Asia constitute one-third of that continent; the population is, however, comparatively speaking thinly scattered; in European Russia it probably amounts to 81,000,000, and in Asiatic to 14,000,000, which give a total of 95,000,000. We can thus form some idea of the briliant prospects of the Russian language, which, instead of being limited to the narrow area of Welsh and Hungarian, is constantly expanding itself. It is fast absorbing the Finnish dialects of the Baltic provinces, and the various languages of Siberia; Lithuanian is yielding before it, and Polish has now almost entirely disappeared from that duchy. But it probably will not so easily absorb the latter, a highly cultivated tongue, which, including Posen, belonging to Prussia, and Galicia to Austria, is still spoken by 9,492,162 persons.[1]

Coast-line, Harbours, and Islands.

Russia possesses a seaboard on the Baltic, the

---

[1] See Budilovich Statisticheskia Tablitzi. St. Petersburg, 1875.

Black Sea, and the Arctic Ocean. It has been the constant aim of her more ambitious sovereigns to extend their dominions so as to reach the sea. The idea of getting a footing upon the Baltic was a favourite one with Ivan the Terrible, and the cause of many of his wars; and it was afterwards developed by Peter the Great, when he constructed the window out of which Russia looks at Europe, as the witty Italian said, and when he extended her frontiers in the south to the Sea of Azov. In fact, nothing seems to have escaped the notice of this ambitious and far-sighted man. It is said that among the Russian archives a plan still exists of an extension of territory in the direction of the Amour, such as has been carried out by the subsequent conquests of Mouraviev. Notes have been added by Peter, who has endorsed the plan, but has appended the word "rano," too early.

The Gulf of Finland is wholly in the possession of Russia, which has the two strongly fortified positions of Kronstadt and Sveaborg. By occupying the Aland Islands, distant only about twenty miles from Stockholm, she is brought into close proximity to Sweden.

The Arctic coast is indented by the White Sea, and contains the port of Archangel, so called because it was founded on the site of the monastery of the Archangel Michael. Here, for the first time, an English ship came to Russia in the year 1553, under the command of Richard Chancellor, but a regular town was not built at Archangel till the year 1637. Close adjoining are the Solovetzkoi Islands, containing a celebrated monastery.

The most valuable portion of the Black Sea coast is the northern section as far E. as Anapa, at the foot of the Caucasus. The coast is very much indented; connected with the mainland by the Isthmus of Perekop is the Crimea, which is narrowed on the W. by the Gulf of Perekop, and on the E. by the Putrid Sea, connected with the Sea of Azov by the Strait of Yenikale, and separated more to the S. by the tongue of Arabat. The chief commercial ports in the Black Sea are Odessa, on a bay midway between the Dnieper and the Dniester; Nikolaiev, at the confluence of the Boug and Dnieper; and Kerch, on the Sea of Azov, and Taganrog, the great emporium of the commerce of the Don.

Mountains and Plateaus.

The only extensive mountain-range is the Oural, with the exception of the small chain of the Yailas in the S. of the Crimea and the Siberian Mountains. All the rest of European Russia is one vast plain. In the eastern part we have the watershed between the basin of the Volga and the rivers that flow to the Arctic Ocean. S. of Lake Ilmen we have the Valdai hills, the highest of which has an elevation of 934 feet.

Rivers, Lakes, Canals, &c.

The great plain of which Russia is composed has two slopes, S.E. to the Caspian and Black Seas, and N.W. to the Baltic and the Arctic Ocean. The influence of the southern line of plateau is observable in the division of the courses of the Don and Dnieper to the S.E. as they pass through it, and in the barrier it places between the Don and the Volga at their nearest point. The lakes of Russia present, on a smaller scale, the features of those of North-America. They are found in close juxta-position, and are intersected by rivers and canals. They are named Ladoga, Onega, Peipous, Saima, Bieloe, Ilmen, and Pskov. Ladoga is the largest lake in Europe, and contains many islands, especially in the northern part, the two most remarkable being Konevetz and Valaam, upon which are monasteries. According to M. Reclus, the abundance of water in these parts is to be explained [2] by the horizontal position of the territory. Onega is very deep, and abounds with little bays; Peipous, as it is called in Esthonian, but Tchoudskoye Ozero, Finnish Lake, as it is named by the Russians, because surrounded by Finnish tribes, was formerly of much greater extent, having been originally in all probability an arm of the sea, which joined the eastern extremity of the Gulf of Finland; Saima is the great lake of Finland, and the tributary of the Ladoga. Lake Ilmen is in reality only a permanent inundation caused by a number of rivers, which meet in the same place.

Direction of the Black Sea.

(*a.*) *Basin of the Dniester.*

This river takes its source in the Carpathians,

[2] Reclus, v. p. 560.

and flowing through the territory of Galicia, which formed part of the ancient kingdom of Poland, passes through Podolia and Bessarabia, and empties itself into the Black Sea. Few rivers of the world have such a tortuous course, and its bed is greatly extended near the source by the salt lakes through which it flows.

(b.) *Basin of the Dnieper.*

This is much greater than that of the Dniester. The Dnieper rises in the marshes near Valdai, and flows from east to west with many windings. It begins to be navigable at Dorogobouzh, passes Smolensk, Mohilev, and Kiev, of which I shall give a more detailed account in a subsequent chapter on the leading cities of Russia. It then flows by Ekaterinoslav, after which begin the cataracts and the large well-wooded islands where the Cossacks established their Sech, or military republic, Ochakov and Kinburn. Tributaries of this river are the Berezina, famous for the passage in the year 1812, the Pripet, the Boug, and the Vorskla, which passes by Poltava, celebrated in history for the defeat of Charles XII. by Peter the Great. Almost the whole of the northern basin of the Dnieper is occupied by the White Russians, who were originally subjects of the principality of Lithuania. The origin of this name has given rise to many disputes, some assigning to the word the meaning of "free," since the territory was independent of the government of the Mongols, others seeing in it an allusion to their dress. Many curious customs prevail among these people, who seem in a greater state of poverty than other parts of Russia.[3] Their songs, however, as shown in the collection of Sheïn and others, are full of tenderness, and exhibit no signs of rudeness. Their country has been unfortunate in having been, during so many centuries, the battle-ground of the wars of the Cossacks, Russians, and Poles. Every year a great number of them leave their homes to be hired in the different workshops of the empire, and they are regarded by the inhabitants of other parts of Russia pretty much as an English villager looks upon an Irish reaper.

On the Desna, a tributary of the Dnieper, is

[3] See Drevnaia i Novaia Rossia.

situated the town of Chernigov, capital of a government of the same name. It has a population of about 10,000, many of whom are Jews; but the place is remarkable for its historical associations, especially on account of the Cherna Mogila (Black Grave) close by, which has been explored by Samokvasov, and described in an early number of the literary journal, "Old and New Russia." According to the theory of many Slavonic scholars, it is in Volinia and White Russia that the original home of the Slavs must be placed. Here tombs are constantly found with the bones of chieftains, their wives, their slaves, and domestic ornaments—such as the mode of burial is described by Herodotus to have been.

It is in White Russia that Schafarik would place the Budini and Neuri of the ancient historian, who are classed by him among the Scythians; but scholars are now pretty well agreed in considering this appellation as a general one, under which many different peoples were included, and thus the varying accounts which we have received as to their physical conditions may be partly reconciled.

(c.) *Basin of the Don.*

The Don, the Tanais of the ancients, rises in the lake of Ivánov.[4] The most important town which it passes is Voronezhe, celebrated as the birthplace of the poets Koltzov and Nikitin.

Isthmus of the Caucasus.

The Black Sea and the Caspian are separated by a great isthmus, which is traversed by a range of mountains, the Caucasus, which in reality are the barrier between Europe and Asia. The scenery is of a grand and startling beauty, and has been celebrated in the verses of the Russian poets Pushkin and Lermontov. There are two principal rivers, of which one, the Kuban, flows into the Black Sea, the other, the Terek,[5] into the Caspian.

Direction of the Caspian Sea.

(a.) *Basin of the Volga.*

The Volga rises in the plains of Valdai, passes

---

[4] It is the fact that the river Don rises in this lake, which has given to it the quaint, humorous name of Don Ivanovich (son of Ivan or John), which occurs so frequently in the folk-songs of the Russians.

[5] See the beautiful verses of Lermontov, "The Gifts of Terek."

Tver, Jaroslav, and Nizhni-Novgorod—celebrated for its fair, on which see a subsequent chapter—Kazan, Simbirsk, Tzaritzin, and empties itself by seventy mouths into the Caspian. Its chief affluents on the right are the Oka, and on the left the Mologa, Cheksna, and Kama.

(*b.*) *Basin of the Oural or Yaik.*

This river is one of the boundaries between Europe and Asia. Its name was changed from Yaik to Oural by order of Catherine II., to efface all recollections of the rebellion of Pougachev, which had been greatly supported by the Yaik Cossacks.

Direction of the Baltic.

Passing by the basins of the Passarge and Pregel, which do not come under Russian geography, a few words must be said of the

(*a.*) *Basin of the Niemen.*

A marshy country abounding in forests, with many small rivers; the soil fertile; the climate unhealthy. A poetical colouring, however, has been thrown over this neglected part of Europe by the ballads of Mickiewicz, and his fine poem, "Pan Tadeusz."

The Niemen rises near Minsk, passes Grodno and Kovno, at which it receives the Vilia, which flows by Vilna, the former capital of Lithuania. From

CROSS AT THE ENTRANCE OF A LITHUANIAN VILLAGE.

Kovno the Niemen passes Tilsit, and finally empties itself into the Kurische Haff.

The basin of the Niemen includes Lithuania, formerly an independent kingdom, which extended almost to the Black Sea, and became celebrated under some of its princes. During the fourteenth century the Lithuanian principality was a dangerous rival of that of Moscow; but the name given to the State in reality only applied to a small portion of the territory; the laws of the country were in White Russian, and the Lithuanian language was never raised above the position of the tongue of peasants. No official documents whatsoever have come down to us in it.[6] In the latter part of last century a Lithuanian clergyman, Christian Donalitius, amused himself in his leisure hours by the composition of several poems dealing with rustic life. These have been published in the present century by Rhesa, Schleicher, and Nesselmann, and the songs of the people have been collected. A great impulse was given to the study of the language by the importance assigned to it in the Indo-European system, by Bopp, in his "Comparative Grammar," which did so much for the tongues of the depressed nationalities of Europe. The admirable Grammar of Schleicher followed; and now the recently-formed Lithuanian Literary Society promises to collect the last gleanings of songs, proverbs, &c., of

[6] See article by Nil Popov in Kriticheskoe Obozrenie.

this interesting people, who are fast disappearing under the combined influences of Russian, German, and Pole; the Lettish language, spoken in the provinces of North Courland, South Livonia, the neighbourhoods of Riga and Mittau,[7] exhibits a later stage of the Lithuanian language, and has probably incorporated Finnish elements. It boasts of a rising literature, and an excellent grammar by Bielenstein. Lithuania is but thinly peopled, the aristocracy being Polish, and the peasantry of Lithuanian origin; the Russians have, however, succeeded in effacing almost entirely the use of the Polish language.[8] The union of Lithuania to Poland was effected by the marriage of Jagiello to Hedvig, or Jadwiga, the daughter of the last king Louis (Ludwik). She is said to have consented to the union on political grounds only, and did not give her hand with her heart in it; that had previously been transferred to a scion of the house of Austria. Terrible stories are told us of the savage hirsuteness and heathen habits of this said Jagiello, who, however, founded a great line in his new

[7] Map of the Slavonic Races by Mirkovich.
[8] See Dr. Perwolf in Bohemian Magazine.

Polish kingdom, succeeding upon the old dynasty of the Piasts, and with the last of his race, Sigismund Augustus II., the glory of Poland culminated. The confederacy of the two kingdoms was further strengthened by the union of Lublin (1569), which was not brought about without a great deal of violence.

(*b*.) *Basin of the Dvina*.

This is a flat country, intersected by lakes, marshes, and little rivers. The Dvina issues from the lakes of Valdai, not far from the sources of the Volga, passes Vitepsk, Polotzk, and Dinabourg, and empties itself into the Baltic at Riga, one of the greatest cities of the empire.

(*c*.) *Basin of the Narva*.

This basin has lake Peipus for the centre, which is increased by many rivers, principally the river Velekaia (Great River), which passes by Pskov, which was one of the Slavonic republics of the Middle Ages, and near which, at Mikhailovskoe, is the burial-place of the most celebrated of Russian poets, Alexander Pushkin. The basin of the Narva comprehends the Russian provinces of Pskov, Livonia, and Ingria. Between the Gulfs of Livonia and Finland is a piece of land jutting out with almost the appearance of a peninsula. This country, which abounds in marshes, is called Esthonia, and its chief city is Revel, one of the most important in the empire. It was founded by the Danes in 1218.

(*d.*) *Basin of the Neva.*

This vast basin has lake Ladoga as its centre. It has a number of tributaries, in the south the Volchov, which brings the waters of lake Ilmen, and passes by Novgorod, originally one of the most celebrated cities of Russia, but now fallen from its greatness and sunk to a mere provincial town. But of this once important place a fuller mention will be made in a subsequent chapter. Its historical position is too great for us to pass it over in a cursory manner. The river Neva flows by Schlusselburg—a fortress connected in many melancholy ways with Russian history; here, among other eminent persons, was detained Eudoxia, the divorced wife of Peter the Great, till her grandson Peter II. ascended the throne—and finally St. Petersburg; but of this great city I shall speak shortly. The basin of the Neva is connected with that of the Volga by several canals. It is this system of canals which furnishes such excellent means of transit for Russian merchandize, and up to a comparatively recent period made up for the want of good roads and railways. Latterly, however, the railway system in Russia has been considerably developed.

Finland.

The Gulfs of Finland and Bothnia encircle a large tract of land almost peninsular in form, a land of rocks and marshes. The chief towns are on the coasts: Viborg which has belonged to the Russians since it was taken by Peter the Great in 1710; Helsingfors, the capital, defended by the fortress, Sveaborg, which has been called the Gibraltar of the Baltic (it was bombarded by the Anglo-French fleet in 1854); Abo (pronounced Obo), the ancient capital of Finland, and formerly the seat of the university. The history of Finland has been a strange one. The bulk of the population belongs to the Ugro-Finnish race, which probably occupied at one time nearly the whole of the northern part of Europe, and a large part of the east of Russia, as is shown by the names of places. They have, however, been gradually receding during the historic period. The culture previous to the occupation by the Russians was wholly Swedish, and this province even gave some good authors to the country, among others Runeberg. It has obtained valuable privileges from the Russians, among which is a kind of local self-government. Since the first conquests of the Swedes in the twelfth century, there have been Scandinavian settlements in the country. At later times Germans and Russians have freely emigrated there. In the north there is a small population of Lapps, and of Gipsies there are considerable numbers, who wander over the country. The population of Finland is given by M. Reclus as 2,020,000.

The great privileges conceded by the Emperor Alexander I. on the conquest of the country, have been further guaranteed by Nicholas and Alexander II. No Finlander can be arbitrarily imprisoned; and when charged with a crime, must be brought to trial at the earliest opportunity. The national representation or Diet has a legislative power in common with the Emperor, and is composed of about 200 members, belonging to the four orders—nobility, clergy, bourgeoisie and peasants. The unanimity of these four orders is necessary for everything relating to the constitution; to privileges and taxes: and no body of troops can be raised without their consent. The professors vote among the clergy.

Direction of the Arctic Ocean.

This country consists of immense steppes, covered during eight months of the year with snow.

(a.) Basin of the Pechora.

This river rises among the Oural mountains, and traverses plains inhabited by the Samoyeds, a people belonging to the Ugro-Finnish race, of whose language a grammar was published by the eminent scholar Castren, at St. Petersburg, in 1854.

(b.) The Northern Dvina.

This river is formed by two branches—the Soukhona, which rises near Vologda, and the Vichegda, which traverses a country almost a desert, and passes Archangel previously described, emptying itself into the White Sea. A canal unites this basin to that of the Volga by the lake of Koubinsk and the Sheskna.

(c.) *Basin of the Onega.*

The lake Onega is the centre of all the waters which come from the Olonetz mountains: it communicates with the White Sea by means of the lakes Sego and Vigo; with the Baltic, by the Svir, the Ladoga and the Neva; by the lake Bieloe (white), and the Volga with the Caspian. Here we see another instance of the complete water communication of Russia.

Asiatic Russia.

Siberia, acquired by the Russians through the energy of the Cossack Yermak, in the reign of Ivan the Terrible, is partly well marked out by natural boundaries. On the north by the Arctic Ocean, by the Pacific Ocean and Behring Strait, and the west by the range of the Oural mountains. In the south the boundary has not yet been fully settled; on the western side it has been carried south of the Amour, and on the eastern side it extends to the Thian Shan mountains. The western portion of Siberia is a vast plain, but in the eastern part the country is much more varied, and we here have the Stanovoi or Verkhoianskoi and Yablonoi mountains. After lake Baikal we come to chains of mountains of great height. The Stanovoi extend throughout the peninsula of Kamchatka. Among them are several volcanoes, of which the following are the most celebrated: Abachinskaia, Koriatzkaia, and Kliouchevskaia. Koriatzkaia has the appearance of a comb, and on its northern side smoke occasionally makes its appearance. To the north of the volcano are some hot springs, and at some versts from it basalt; Kliouchevskaia has a conical form, and almost every year throws up a great quantity of ashes, which are sometimes carried by the wind to a distance of two hundred versts. Asiatic Russia is one-third larger than all Europe: besides Siberia, it consists of the Caucasian provinces and Russian Turkestan, the inhabitants of which are wandering Kirghis tribes, and to their territory has been added the northern parts of Kokan and

Bokhara. The chief town of this new territory is Tashkend.

Direction of the Arctic Ocean.
Mountains.

(1.) The Siberian range, extending from W. to E., consisting of the Altai, Sayansk, and Daourian mountains.

(*a.*) The Altai mountains extend along the southern divisions of the governments of Tobolsk and Tomsk, and unite with the mountains of Okhost by means of the Yablonoi and Stanovoi range. They begin about the sources of the Tobol and Ishim, and terminate about the river Kemchik, a tributary of the Yenisei.

(*b.*) The Sayansk mountains extend between the Yenisei and lake Baikal to the distance of 1260 versts; a continuation of them, stretching along the western shore of lake Baikal, is named after the lake.

(*c.*) The Daourian stretch from the Sagansk mountains as far as the Yablonoi ridge, and extend to China.

(2.) The Siberian range, extends in a north-eastern direction.

(*a.*) The Yablonoi mountains are a continuation of the Sayansk range.

(*b.*) The Stanovoi, extend along the western and northern shores of the sea of Okhosk, a continuation of the Yablonoi range.

The Kamchatka mountains separate the peninsula of that name into two parts, the eastern and western. The southern part terminates with Cape Lopatka.

Rivers.

(*a.*) The Obi descends from the Little Altai, and passing by Berezov, empties itself into the Gulf of Obi. The town of Berezov has earned an historical celebrity from its connexion with so many eminent Russian exiles.

"The melancholy scenery is covered with a shroud of snow during eight months: the severe frosts sometimes reach a pitch of forty-five degrees, the cold stops the breath, and changes the vapour breathed out into rime; birds fall dead; the panes of glass in the windows crack; the earth and ice show great fissures. The weather is remarkable for its changeableness; the air is damp and misty; the sky is always covered with dark clouds, and violent storms are very frequent. The only means of safety for the man or animal overtaken by them is to lie in the snow and wait their end, sometimes for a whole day. The nights are prolonged and gloomy, only at times the darkness is relieved by the magnificent appearance of the polar sky—the Aurora Borealis. The silence of the desert prevails in the little town, which is always half dark and covered with snow. The coniferous trees alone are found—the cedar,[9] the fir, and the pine—these reach a great height and keep their verdure, and are the only enlivening features amidst the general gloom."[1]

This description will convey a picture of the Arctic scenery. Berezov was founded in the year 1593, in the time of the Tzar Feodore, to establish the Russian rule over the Ostiaks. It takes its name from the neighbouring Ostiak village Sougmont-Bozhe, the meaning of which is Birch Town.

(*b.*) The Tom, which passes Tomsk.

(*c.*) The Irtysh, which passes by Semipalatinsk, Petropavlovsk; and Tobolsk, the capital of Siberia, which will be described in another part of this

---

[9] The Siberian cedar or stone-pine.
[1] Shubinski, Historical Sketches and Tales, p. 40.

work. The Yenisei passes by Krasnoyarsk (Red Cliff), and discharges itself into the gulf named after it, receiving many tributaries on its way. The Lena rises in lake Baikal, and empties itself into the Arctic Ocean, near a small archipelago of islands.

Direction of the Pacific.

The only important river to be mentioned here is the Amour, which separates the Russian and Chinese empires.

Of course, in a country of such a wide extent as Russia, we must be prepared for great diversities of climate. There are four zones :—(1) The Arctic Zone, where the rivers are frozen for about nine months; here are only mosses and dwarf shrubs. (2) The Cold Zone, between the Arctic Circle and the fifty-seventh parallel, in which the rivers are frozen for about six months; here are vast forests of pine and birch, and rye, oats, and barley grow, in increasing quantities, from N. to S. (3) The Temperate Zone, between the fifty-seventh and fiftieth parallels; chief productions: wheat, hemp, and millet. (4) The Warm Zone, which has a very cold winter and a very warm summer; this is the region of the steppes; in the southern part the temperature is so hot that wine is produced (*e.g.* in the Crimea). The richest parts of Russia, are the so-called black lands, including the mid basin of the Volga and the Ukraine. This zone of black land extends from the S.W. to the N.W., like an isthmus between the Carpathian and Oural mountains. In the N. some little islands of black land are scattered about, in the governments of Viatka, Kazan, Vladimir, and Chernigov.[2] In these parts the steppes teem with animal life, and those of the Dnieper and the Don are especially the lands for the keeping of bees. Originally, in the Ukraine, honey was found not only in the trunks of trees, but in the cavities of the earth, especially the steep banks of rivers and ravines. The most barren are the regions of the extreme N., and the swamps between the Pripet and the Niemen. The upper basin of the former river, which is one of the principal affluents of the Dnieper, is almost entirely marsh, but when the water has once been got rid of these regions may be transformed into lands of extreme fertility. The whole country is a

[2] Reclus, Nouvelle Geographic Universelle, v. p. 446.

labyrinth of lakes, of marshes, of turbaries, and of forests, which constitute the government of Pinsk. Restrained on the southern side by the granite rocks of Volînia, the waters have been unable to flow properly in the basin of the Dnieper; they have accumulated in the middle of the lower lands where they used to form a lake, but are now a collection of sluggish streams, the banks of which can be no longer recognized on account of the number of reeds and water-plants.[3]

There is abundance of timber, large tracts of the country consisting of vast forests. Its mineral wealth is also great, especially in the region of the Upper Oural mountains extending as far as Bogoslovsk. Among the minerals and precious stones found are sapphire, emerald, amethyst, agate, rhodonite, the rock crystal, jasper, chrysoberyl, and black tourmalin. Diamonds have also been found, but in insignificant quantities. The chief treasures, however, of the Oural mines are gold, platina, copper, and iron. According to some authorities there is but little coal, a small bed of inferior quality having been

[3] Reclus, v. 450.

found between the rivers Dnieper and Don.[4] The traveller on the railways will everywhere see large stacks of wood ready for consumption, this being almost invariably used as fuel for the engines. Of cereals, rye—except in the steppes and the Arctic regions—is easily grown throughout the whole country. Barley and oats are extensively cultivated, and wheat in the Ukraine. Besides these, there are millet and maize. No country produces so much flax and hemp as Russia. Tobacco is also grown in the Ukraine; very little fruit is grown in the more northern parts of Russia, with the exception of wild cherries and inferior apples; no fruits grow N. of 56° N. latitude. In the most southern parts of the country are produced peaches, apricots, walnuts, and in the Crimea even pomegranates. Grapes are cultivated along the lower course of the Don, and in the Crimea. Most of the common vegetables are abundant, and

[4] M. Reclus, however, writes as follows (p. 870): "L'étendue des terrains houillers, en Pologne, dans la Russie centrale, dans la région du Donetz, n'a pas encore été reconnue d'une manière complète, mais elle est certainement beaucoup plus considérable que celle des houillères de tout autre pays d'Europe.

hops in some places. The domestic animals of Russia are nearly the same as the English. Sheep and cattle are numerous; and there are also several breeds of horses, the small and wiry ones being very celebrated, and in great use among the Cossacks. Goats and hogs are in abundance, and the tribes that wander about the steppes also employ camels.

In the extreme northern part of the country are reindeer. Of wild animals there is the bison, or auerochs; in the northern forests, elks, deer, hares, and wild hogs, bears, badgers, wolves, foxes, ermines, otters, and squirrels. In the steppes are wild asses and antelopes. The birds which are met with in Russia are almost identical with those found in England. Fish of all kinds is abundant in the rivers and seas.

CHAPTER II.

ETHNOLOGY.

THE vast Empire of Russia, as may be readily imagined, is peopled by many different races. These may ethnologically be catalogued as follows :

1. Slavonic races, the most important in numbers and culture. Under this head may be classified :—

(1.) The Great Russians, or Russians properly so called, especially occupying the Governments round about Moscow, and from thence scattered in the N. to Novgorod and Vologda, on the S. to Kiev and Voronezh, on the E. to Penza, Simbirsk, and Viatka, and on the W. to the Baltic provinces. Moreover, the Great Russians, as the ruling race, are to be found in small numbers in all quarters of the Empire. They amount to about 40,000,000.

(2.) Little Russians (Malorossiani), dwelling south

of the Russians, upon the shores of the Black Sea. These, together with the Rusniaks, amount to 16,370,000.

The Cossacks come under these two races.

To the Great Russian belong the Don Cossacks, with those sprung from them—the Kouban, Stavropol, Khoperski, Volga, Mosdok, Kizlarski, and Grebenski.

To the Little Russian: the Malorossiiski, with those sprung from them—the Zaporoghian, Black Sea (Chernomorski), and those of Azov and of the Danube. In a subsequent part of this work I shall take occasion to say a few words on the history of the Cossacks and their military republics, rendered so famous by the Taras Boulba of the novelist Gogol; and their rich collections of national songs, which have found editors in Messrs. Dragomanov and Antonovich.

(3.) The White Russians, inhabiting the Western Governments. Their number amounts to 4,000,000.

(4.) Poles, living in the former Kingdom of Poland and the Western Governments of the Empire. Their number amounts to 5,000,000.

(5.) Servians, Bulgarians, and other Slavs, inhabiting especially Bessarabia and the country called New Russia. Their number reaches 150,000.

The Non-Slavonic races comprise either original inhabitants of the country who have been subdued by the Russians, or later comers. Among races originally inhabiting the country, and subjugated by the Russians, are included—the Lithuanians and Letts, the Finns, the Samoyeds, the Mongol-Manzhurians, the races of Eastern Siberia, the Turko-Tartar, the Caucasian, the German, and the Hebrew.

1. The Lithu-Lettish race inhabits the country between the Western Dvina and the Nieman. In numbers they do not amount to more than 3,000,000. The Lithu-Lettish population is divided into the two following branches:—

(*a*.) The Lithuanians[1] properly so called (including the Samogitans or Zhmudes), who inhabit the Governments of Vilno, Kovno, Courland, and the northern parts of those of Augustovo and Grodno (1,900,000).

---

[1] For a good representation of the settlements of the Lithuanians (who spread partly into the Prussian dominions), see the map prefixed to Kurschat's "Lithuanian Grammar."

(*b.*) The Letts, who inhabit the Governments of Courland, Vitebsk, Livonia, Kovno, Pskov, and St. Petersburg (1,100,000).

2. The Finnish race—known in the old Slavonic chronicles under the name of Chouds—at one time inhabited all the north-eastern part of Russia. The Finns, according to the place of their habitation, are divided into four groups:—the Baltic Finns, the Finns in the Governments of the Volga, the Cis-Oural and the Trans-Oural Finns.

(*a.*) The Baltic Finns: the Chouds (in the Governments of Novgorod and Olonetz); the Livonians (in Courland); the Esthonians (in the Governments of Esthonia, Livonia, Vitebsk, Pskov, and St. Petersburg); the Lopari (in northern Finland and in the Government of Archangel); the Corelians (in the Governments of Archangel, Novgorod, Olonetz, St. Petersburg, Tver, and Jaroslav); Evremeiseti (in the Governments of Novgorod and St. Petersburg), Savakoti, Vod, and Izhora.

(*b.*) To the Finns of the Governments of the Volga, who have become almost lost in the Russians, belong the Cheremisians (in the Governments of Kazan, Viatka, Kostroma, Nizhni-Novgorod, Orenburg, and Perm).

(*c.*) To the Cis-Uralian Finns, who occupy the country from the borders of Finland to the Oural, belong the Permiaks (in the Governments of Viatka and Perm); Ziranians (in the Governments of Archangel and Vologda); Votiaks (in the Governments of Viatka and Kazan); and Vogoulichi (in the Government of Perm).

(*d.*) Among the Trans-Oural Finns are also to be numbered the Ziranians and Vogoulichi (the first in the Government of Tobolsk, and the second in the Governments of Tobolsk and Tomsk); and the Ostiaks, who, according to the places of their habitation, are called Obski and Berezovski.

The Finns amount altogether to 2,100,000.

3. The Samoyeds, in number 70,000, live in the territory extending from the White Sea to the Yenesei; to these belong the Samoyeds properly so called, the Narîmski, and Yenesei Ostiaks, the Olennie Choukchi, &c.

4. The Mongolo-Manzhourian race, amounting to 400,000. Among this race may be remarked the Mongolians properly so called, on the Selenga;

KALMUCK VILLAGE.

the Kalmucks, a nomad people in the Government of Astrakhan, as also in Tomsk, in the country of the Don Cossacks, and partly in the Government of Stavropol. The Kalmucks appeared first on the eastern confines of Russia in the year 1630. About a century later we find them become the regular subjects of the Tzar. They seem, however, to have found the Russian yoke irksome, and resolved to return to their original home on the coasts of Lake Balkach, and at the foot of the Altai Mountains. Nearly the whole nation, amounting to almost 300,000 persons, began their march in the winter of 1770-71. The passage of this vast host lasted for weeks, but the rear were prevented from escaping by the Kirghiz and Cossacks, who intercepted them. They were compelled to remain in Russia, where their territory was more accurately defined than had been done previously. The Kalmucks are obliged to serve with the Cossack troops, but their duties are mostly confined to looking after the cattle and horses which accompany the army.[2] Their religion is Buddhism, and a conspicuous object in the aouls, or temporary villages which

[2] Reclus, p. 69.

they construct, is the pagoda. Their personal appearance is by no means prepossessing—small eyes and high cheekbones, with scanty hair of a very coarse texture. In every sense of the word they are still strictly nomads; their children and tents are carried by camels, and in a few hours their temporary village, or oulous, is established. To these also belong the Bouriats, by Lake Baikal; the Toungusians from the Yenesei to the Amour; the Lamouts, by the Sea of Okhotsk; and the Olentzi, in the Government of Irkutsk.

5. Races of Eastern Siberia: the Koriaks, living in the north-eastern corner of Siberia; the Youka-girs, in the territory of Yakutsk; the Kamchadales, in Kamchatka. Their number amounts to 500,000.

6. The Turko-Tatar race amount in number to 3,000,000. To their branch belong the Chouvashes, in the Governments of Orenburg, Simbursk, Saratov, and Samara; the Mordvinians, in the same Governments as the Chouvashes,[3] and in those of Tambov, Penza, and Nizhni-Novgorod; the Tatars

---

[3] Some writers consider the Chouvashes to belong to the Finnish race.

LESGHIAN.

of the Crimea and Kazan; the Nagais, on the Kouban and Don; the Mestcheriaki, in the Governments of Orenburg, Perm, Saratov, and Viatka; Koumki, in the Caucasus; Kirghizi, Yakouti, on the Lena; Troukhmentzi and Khivintzi; Karakalpaks (lit. Black Caps), Teleoûti, in the Government of Tomsk, Siberia.

7. The Caucasian races inhabiting Georgia, the valleys and the defiles of the Caucasian Mountains have different appellations and different origins. Among them may be noticed the Armenians, Georgians, Circassians, Abkhasians, Lesghians, Osetintzi, Chechentzi, Kistentzi, Toushi, and others. Their number is about 2,000,000.

The languages of the Caucasus must be regarded as a group distinct both from the Aryan and Semitic families. They are agglutinative, and are divided into two branches.

(*a*.) The Northern Division, extending along the northern slopes of the Caucasus, between the Caspian and the northern shores of the Black Sea, as far as the Straits of Yenikale; its subdivisions are Lesghian, Kistian, and Circassian, each with its dialects. Formerly the Circassians numbered about 500,000, but large numbers of them emigrated to European Turkey, where they were dexterously planted by the government to impede the social progress of their Bulgarian and Greek subjects.

(*b.*) The Southern Division, comprising Georgian, Suanian, Mingrelian, and Lazian.[1]

8. The German race, in number about 1,000,000. The Germans are chiefly in the Baltic provinces, in the Government of St. Petersburg, in the Grand Duchy of Finland, and the colonies, especially those on the lower Volga, the Don, the Crimea, and New Russia. The Germans have acquired great influence throughout the country; they are represented in the court, in the army, and in the administration. Here also may be mentioned the Swedes, amounting to 286,000.

9. The Jews inhabit especially the former Kingdom of Poland, the Western Governments, and the Crimea. Their number amounts to 3,000,000. Among the Jews the Karaimite are noticeable, living in the Governments of Vilno, Volînia, Kovno, Kherson, and the Taurida. Among the

See Hovelacque, "The Science of Language," English ranslation, p. 136.

Europeans and Asiatics who have come in later times to settle in Russia, are Greeks, amounting to 75,000, in the Governments of New Russia and Chernigov; French, Italians, and Englishmen, in the capitals and chief commercial towns; Wallachians or Moldavians (now generally included under the name of Roumanians), in Bessarabia; Albanians; Gipsies, especially in the territory of Bessarabia, amounting to 50,000; Persians, to 10,000, &c.

CHAPTER III.

LANGUAGE, LITERATURE, AND ART.

I DO not propose on the present occasion to discuss the various languages of all the peoples who inhabit the Russian Empire. I shall content myself mainly with the Slavonic branch.

I have already spoken of the Lithuanian and Lettish: and of the vast Ugro-Finnish family a few words may be said. The languages of the last group, sometimes called Uralo-Altaic, are classed as agglutinative, and may be arranged in five sub-divisions—Samoyedic, Finnic, Tataric, Mongolian, and Tungusian. Of these the most interesting is the Finnic group, all the languages of which are spoken in Russia, with the exception of Magyar and some dialects of Lappic. The philology of these tongues had been very much neglected till recently; but the labours of Kellgren, Weske, and Donner, have greatly advanced the study. Especially valuable are the "Untersuchungen zur Vergleichenden Grammatik des Finnischen Sprachstammes" of Weske, and the "Vergleichendes Wörterbuch der Finnish-Ugrischen Sprachen" of Donner. The latter makes the following five sub-groups of this Finnish branch:—

West Finnic: Suomi, Karelian, Vepsic Livonian, Krewinian, Esthonian, Wotic.

Lappic.

Finno-Permian: Zîranian, Permian, Votiak.

Volga-Finnic: Mordvinian, Cheremissian.

Ugric: Magyaric, Vogulic, Ostiak.[1]

Before the occupation of the country by the Russians, every educated Finlander aspired to speak Swedish, and the Finnish language was treated with contempt. A certain status, however, was given to the language by the translation of the Bible in 1548. Lectures are now given in Finnish in the University of Helsingfors, and since 1868 all the new schoolmasters and Government employés

---

[1] See Hovelacque's (English edition, p. 90) "Science of Language."

must be acquainted with it. In 1849, the "Kalevala," a kind of Finnish epic, taken down from the lips of the people, was published by Lönrot. He had collected the verses by traversing all Finland, and the Russian Governments of Olonetz and Arkhangel. Soon afterwards this poem was translated into Swedish by Castren; and there is a French translation, which will make it more accessible to readers in the west of Europe. An account of the "Kalevala," with a short summary, is also given by Dr. Latham, in his "Russian and Turk," p. 271. The handiest edition for the Finnish scholar is that published at Helsingfors, in 1862.

The Slavonic family of languages is thus divided by Schleicher:—

South-Eastern Branch.

I.

1. Old Bulgarian . Modern Bulgarian.
2. Russian . . . { Little Russian, Red Russian or Ruthenian.
3. Servian or Croatian. } Slovenish.

II.

1. Polish . . . . { Various dialects, including Kashubish.
2. Čech . . . . . Slovakish.
3. Lusatian . . . { Upper Dialect.
   Wendish . . . { Lower Dialect.
4. Polabish . . . (Extinct.)

The most ancient form of Slavonic is the Ecclesiastical language, so called because it is employed in the church services. It has long ceased to be spoken. There is still a great contention as to whether this language is most exactly represented by the modern Bulgarian or the Slovenish. The great supporter of the latter opinion at the present time is Professor Micklosich, of Vienna, but against it are to be cited Schleicher, Schafarik, and J. Schmidt.

Of the Russian there are the following chief dialects—Great, Little, and White Russian. The Great Russian, is the literary and official language of the Empire. In its structure it is highly synthetic, having three genders and seven cases, and the nouns and adjectives being fully inflected.

Its great peculiarity (which it shares in common with all the Slavonic languages) is the structure of the verbs, which are divided into so-called "aspects," which modify the meaning just as the Latin terminations sco, urio, and ito, only the forms are developed into a more perfect system. The letters employed are the Cyrillian, held to have been invented by St. Cyril in the ninth century. They are on the whole well adapted to express the many sounds of the Russian alphabet, for which the Latin letters would be wholly inadequate, and must perforce be employed in some such uncouth combinations as those which communicate a grotesque appearance to Polish. It would be out of place here to discuss the Ecclesiastical Slavonic employed in so many of the early writings composed in Russian. I shall proceed to speak of the literature in Russian properly so-called. The great epochs of this will be—

1. From the earliest times to the reign of Peter the Great.

2. From the reign of Peter the Great to our own time.

The Russians, like the rest of the Slavonic

peoples, are very rich in national songs, many (as one may judge from the allusions found in them) going back to a remote antiquity. For a long time, and especially during the period of French influence, these productions were neglected. In the last twenty years, however, they have been assiduously collected by such indefatigable antiquaries as Bezsonov, Kirievski, Rîbnikov, Hilferding, and others. The Russian legendary poems are called Bîlini (literally, tales of old time), and may be most conveniently divided into the following classes :—

1. That of the earlier heroes.
2. The Cycle of Vladimir.
3. The Royal or Moscow Cycle.

To these a fourth may be added, that of the Cossacks; but as their songs are in the Malo-Russian, a dialect or language spoken over a great part of southern Russia, I shall treat of them separately.

The early heroes are of a half-mythical type, and perform prodigies of valour. To this class belong Volga Vseslavich, Mikoula Selianinovich and Sviatogor. Volga undergoes all kinds of transformations. We have here the rude Titanic forces found in all the early mythologies. M. Rambaud, in his "La Russie Epique,"[2] compares Sviatogor with Proteus and Loki. Like them he can assume any appearance he pleases; he becomes an eagle, a serpent, and a wild beast. In the latter guise he succeeds in catching many wild animals, and clothes the young men of his drouzhina, or company, in their skins.

One of the most interesting of these heroes is the peasant Mikoula Selianinovich, a character that figures very much in Slavonic legends, having a great deal in common with the mythical Piast and Premysl among the Poles and Čechs. He is a kind of Hercules, in the person of whom physical strength is glorified. Neither Volga nor any of his drouzhina can lift the hero's plough; he himself with a single touch raises it from the earth, and hurls it to the clouds.

The great glory of the Cycle of Vladimir is Ilya Murometz. The bîlinas are filled with his

---

[2] A very interesting work. Those who are curious about early Russian literature should certainly consult Mr. Ralston's "Russian Folk-songs" and "Folk-tales."

magnificent exploits, either alone or in the company of Sviatogor. On one occasion he visits the father of the latter hero, who, being blind, wishes to touch the hand of Ilya, to see whether it has the champion's true vigour. Ilya takes a piece of iron, makes it red hot, and offers it to the veteran, who, grasping it so tightly that he forces sparks to fly in all directions, exclaims, "Thou hast a strong hand and hot blood: thou art a true hero."

The character of Vladimir is represented as genial and hospitable; but we do not find any particular acts of bravery assigned to him, nor do we trace any of the aristocratic notions of the West with regard to precedence at his banquets. On the seat of the heroes sit also Stavre, the rich boyar, and Alesha, the son of a priest, and Ivan, the son of a merchant, and finally Ilya Murometz, a peasant. Equal honour is given to all guests; the court of the prince is always open; at the entrance are oaken pillars, and in the pillars steel rings are fixed. When a warrior arrives, he fastens his horse to one of these rings, and forthwith enters the presence-chamber, first bowing to the sacred picture, then to the prince and princess, and after that to each side of the hall, where the assembled guests are sitting. The Grand Duke then inquires of the new comer concerning his parentage, and causes to be offered to him " a bull's horn of sweet mead." This the hero rapidly drains, and empties the goblet—which is celebrated as a glorious achievement.[3] This feat accomplished, the guest takes his place at the banquet with the others. Afterwards, at that hour when "the day is half spent and the feast is half spent," Prince Vladimir proposes some deed of prowess.

The Cycle of Novgorod is not so rich as that of Kiev; but the former city must have attained a magnificence at an earlier period, of which there is no historical record. The voice of tradition, and the discoveries made in those tombs which have been examined in the district, all point to the same conclusion. In the early chronicles we get an account of the luxury and turbulence of the inhabitants of the great Slavonic Republic. Novgorod was fortunate in its geographical position, not alone as the great emporium of trade, but as being removed from the devastation of the Tartars. Its

[3] Compare the Frithiof Saga.

independence, however, was crushed by the vigorous centralizing measures of Ivan III., to whom the consolidation of the Russian power may be attributed. In 1487 an end was put for ever to the Vech, the National Assembly; and the bell which had previously summoned the citizens to the council, was triumphantly carried off to Moscow. It is to the period of the great aristocracy, commenced by Ivan III., and perfected by his successors, that the bîlinas of the fourth period belong.

The chief events which they celebrate are, the taking of Kazan in 1552, and the conquest of Siberia by Yermak. In spite of all his atrocities, the memory of Ivan IV. is not regarded with any dislike by the Russians. There is a tendency in these poems to repress all disagreeable details, and to dwell only on the conquests and glories of the Tzar. Here and there we have the lay of some traitor, who has been sentenced to death, and thanks the sovereign for his kindness to him, even though he has ordered his rebellious head to be cut from his sturdy shoulders. A subject of song at this period was the infamous Maliouta Skourlatovich, who aided and abetted the Tzar in so many of his atrocities, and stood in the same relation to him as Tristan l'Hermite to Louis XI. Indeed Ivan bears a very great similarity to the last-mentioned monarch, in his duplicity, his cruelty, his vigorous personal government, and the suspicion with which he regarded all who surrounded him. Nor must his superstition be forgotten. Just as Louis hid himself in his loop-holed and well-barricaded castle of Plessy, so did Ivan retire to the gloomy shades of his residence at Alexandrovski. The bílinas relating to Ivan and his predecessors have been orally communicated, and have lived for centuries on the lips of the peasants. It is interesting for Englishmen to know that the first ever committed to writing were preserved by one Richard James, an Oxford graduate, who was in Russia in 1619 as chaplain to the embassy. These valuable manuscripts are preserved among the Ashmolean Collection, and, as may readily be imagined, have not escaped the notice of Russian editors. An account of these poems may be found in Bouslaev's "Historical Sketches of Russian National Literature and Art" (Istoricheskie Ocherki Rousskoi Narodnoi Slovesnosti i Iskousstva), and some extracts in his valuable Russian Chrestomathy, in which specimens of the language are arranged historically from the Ostromir Gospels to the end of the seventeenth century—a work of the highest importance to the student of this most interesting language.

The national songs are carried on through the troublous times of Boris Godunov, and the false Dimitri, to the days of Peter the Great, when they seem to have acquired new vigour on account of the military achievements of the regenerator of his country. Nor are they extinct in our own time, for we find exploits of Napoleon, especially his disastrous expedition to Russia, made the subject of verse. The interest, however, of these legendary poems fades away as we advance into later days. The number of minstrels is rapidly diminishing; and Riabanin and his companions among the Great Russians, and Ostap Veresai among the Malo-Russians, will probably be the last of these generations of rhapsodists, who have transmitted their traditional chants from father to son, from tutor to pupil. A great feature in Russian literature is the collection of chronicles, which begin with Nestor, monk of the Pestcherski Cloister at Kiev, who was born about A.D. 1056, and died about 1116. Nestor knew the Byzantine historians well. The early part of his work is a strange medley of fact and legend; and so highly coloured and poetical is the style in many places, that one suspects that he has bodily incorporated bîlini which are now forgotten, as the Polish historians Gallus, Kadlubek, and Dlugosz did. In very few instances, however, are we able to ascertain the names of the authors of these compilations, which will remind the English reader of the Anglo-Saxon chronicle more than anything else. There is the same curious mixture of the most trivial and most important events, the same juxtaposition of highly wrought narrative with bald and prosaic details. The chain of the chronicles extends in almost unbroken continuity to the days of Alexis Mikhailovich, the father of Peter the Great. A good edition of these works was published at St. Petersburg in 1846, but they more properly belong to Palæoslavonic than to Russian literature. During the time when Russia groaned under the yoke of the Mongols the nation remained silent, except here and there, perhaps, in some legendary song, sung among peasants, and destined subsequently to be gathered from oral tradition by a Rîbnikov and a Hilferding. Such literature as was cultivated formed the recreation of the monks in their cells. A new era, however, was to come. Ivan III. established the autocracy, and made Moscow the centre of the new government. The Russians naturally looked to Constantinople as the centre of their civilization; and even when the city was taken by the Turks its influence did not cease. Many learned Greeks fled to Russia, and found an hospitable reception in the dominions of the Grand Duke. During the reigns of Ivan the Terrible and his immediate successors, although the material progress of the country was considerably advanced, and a strong Government founded, yet little was done for learning. Simeon Polotzki (1628-80) tutor to the Tzar Feodor, son of Alexis, was an indefatigable writer of religious and educational books, but his productions can now only interest the antiquarian. The verses composed by him on the new palace built by the Tzar Alexis, at Kolomenski are deliciously quaint. Some extracts are given by Bouslaev, in the Chrestomathy previously mentioned. Of a more important character is the sketch of the Russian Government, and the habits of the people, written by one Koshikin (or Kotoshikin—for the name is found in both forms), a renegade diak or secretary, which, after having lain for a long time in manuscript in the library of Upsala, in Sweden, was edited in 1840 by the Russian historian Soloviev. Kotoshikin terminated a life of strange vicissitudes by perishing at the hands of the public executioner at Stockholm, about 1669.

With the reforms of Peter the Great commences an entirely new period in the history of Russian literature, which was now to be under Western influence. The epoch was inaugurated by Lomonosov, the son of a poor fisherman of Archangel, who forms one of the curious band of peasant authors—of very various merit, it must be confessed—who present such an unexpected phenomenon in Russian literature. Occasionally we have men of real genius, as in the cases of Koltzov, Nikitin, and Shevchenko, the great glory of southern Russia; sometimes, perhaps, a man whose abilities have been overrated, as in the instance of Slepoushkin.

Lomonosov, having exhausted the scanty stock of literature which the miserable village where he lived could furnish, resolved to make his way to the great capital, Moscow. This he effected upon a waggon laden with fish, and as a candidate for learning knocked at the doors of an educational establishment of which he had heard mention amid the snows of his dreary northern home. He was afterwards sent, at the expense of the Government, to finish his studies in Germany. He resided for some time at Marburg, but falling into debt there, resolved to betake himself secretly to Lubeck, and from thence to sail to Russia. On his way a droll adventure befell him; at Dusseldorf he met with a Prussian recruiting officer, who, delighted with the ample bulk and vigorous thews of the Russian student, was determined to add him to the number of his conscripts. He accordingly persuaded Lomonosov to drink with him: the future poet became stupefied by his copious libations, and on waking up found himself decorated with the Prussian uniform. From the consequences of this disagreeable meeting he was only saved by the intervention of the Russian ambassador. Lomonosov meets us an indefatigable man of letters. His writings are on a variety of topics: we have essays, plays, epics, lyrical poems, and many others; but, perhaps, he was more successful in natural science than any other subjects treated of by his versatile pen. Such a man frequently appears in the infancy of a country's literature. The ground seemed altogether unoccupied for Lomonosov. The old Byzantine culture was absolutely dead; it remained for the new author, following in the path of the labours of Peter, to introduce his countrymen to the culture of the West. He did much to improve the language, reducing it to rules by his careful grammar, which, although not based on sound philological principles, was for a long time regarded as a model for all future attempts. He had to mark more accurately than had hitherto been observed the exact limits which separated the forms of modern Russian from the Ecclesiastical Slavonic. Lomonosov is more praised than read by his countrymen. His turgid odes, stuffed with classical allusions, in praise of Anne and Elizabeth, are still committed to memory by pupils at educational establishments. His panegyrics are certainly fulsome, but probably no worse than those of Boileau in praise of Louis XIV., who grovelled without the excuse of the imperfectly educated Scythian. The reign of Catherine II. (1762-96) saw the rise of a whole generation of court poets. The great maxim, " Un Auguste peut aisément faire un Virgile," was seen in all its absurdity in semi-barbarous Russia. These wits were supported by the Empress and her immediate *entourage*, to whom their florid productions were ordinarily addressed. In the strict sense of the word there was no reading public in Russia; only in the dreary huts of the peasants through the long winter nights, the wandering rhapsodist kept up the tradition of their poetical legends, of which we have previously spoken. But the Gallicized courtier of the epoch of Catherine regarded these productions with contempt as the babble of savages. They were only to be collected in the present century, when the great reaction against the pseudo-classical school had set in. As I do not propose to fatigue my readers with a mere catalogue of names uncouth to Western ears, I shall not dilate upon the Kheraskovs, Ozerovs, Sumarokovs, and their satellites.

From Byzantine traditions, from legends of saints, confused chronicles, and orthodox hymnologies, Russia was to pass, by one of the most violent changes ever witnessed in the literature of any country, into epics moulded upon the "Henriade," and tedious odes in the style of Boileau and Jean Baptiste Rousseau. Oustrialov, the historian, truly characterizes most of the voluminous writers of this epoch, as mediocre verse-makers : he has reason, however, for claiming merit in the cases of Bogdanovich, Khemnitzer, Von Vizin, Dmitriev, and Derzhavin. Bogdanovich wrote a very pretty lyric piece, styled "Dushenka," based on the story of Cupid and Psyche, and partly imitated from Lafontaine, but with a sportive charm about the verse which will preserve it from becoming obsolete. With Khemnitzer begin the fabulists. But I shall reserve my remarks upon this species of literature, and its Russian votaries, till I come to Krîlov, who may be said to be one of the few Slavonic authors who have gained a reputation beyond the limits of their own country. In Denis Von Vizin, born at Moscow, but, as his name shows, of German extraction, Russia saw a writer of genuine national comedy. Hitherto she had been obliged to content herself with poor imitations of Molière. His two plays, the "Brigadier" and the "Minor" (Nedorosl), have much original talent. No such vigorous representations of character appeared again on the stage till "The Misfortune of being too Clever" (Gore ot Ouma), of Griboiedov, and the "Revisor" of Gogol. Dmitriev deserves perhaps no more than a passing mention. He enjoyed great popularity in his time, and there is an elegance and finish about his odes which did much to improve the style of Russian literature; they lack, however, originality, and are as frigid as the productions of Mason, and others of our own writers at the close of the last century. Russia still looked to classical models.

The name of Derzhavin is spoken of with reverence among his countrymen: he was the laureate of the epoch of Catherine, and had a fresh ode for every new military glory. There is much fire and vigour in his productions, and he could develope the strength and flexibility of his native language which can be made as expressive and concise as Greek. Perhaps, however, we get a little tired of the endless perfections of Felitza, the name under which he celebrates the Empress Catherine, a woman who—whatever her private faults may have been—did a great deal for Russia.

In Nicholas Karamzin appeared the first Russian historian who can properly claim the title. His poems are now almost forgotten: here and there we come upon a solitary lyric in a book of extracts. His tales, in which the sentimentalism of Sterne, and the "Sorrows of Young Werther," found a Slavonic echo, have also sunk into partial oblivion. His "History of the Russian Empire," however, is a work of extensive research, and must always be quoted with respect by Slavonic scholars. Unfortunately, it only extends to the election of Michael Romanov. This was the first regular attempt at compiling Russian history, for the production of Tatistchev was merely a rude sketch, wanting both in critical power and elegance of style. Karamzin was followed by the indefatigable Nicholas Polevoi, son of a Siberian merchant, who left hardly any species of literature untouched. His "History of the Russian People," however, did not add to his reputation, and is now almost forgotten. In later times both these authors have been eclipsed by such writers as Soloviev and Kostomarov. A new and more critical school of Russian historians has sprung up ; but for the early history of the Slavonic peoples, the great work is still Schafarik's "Slavonic Antiquities," first published in the Bohemian language, and more familiar to scholars in the West of Europe in its German version. I shall have occasion to speak of the progress of Russian historical studies shortly. With the breaking up of the old forms of government caused by the French Revolution, came the dislocation of the old conventional modes of thought. Classicism in literature was dead, having weighed like an incubus upon the fancy and fresh life of many generations. England and Germany were at the head of the new movement, which was at a later period to be joined by France. The influence was to extend also to Russia, and may be said to date from the reign of Alexander I. It was headed by Zhukovski, who was rather a fluent translator than an original poet. He has given excellent versions of Schiller, Güthe, Moore, and Byron, and has better enriched the literature of his country in this way than by his original productions. He had however, some lyric fire of his own; the ode entitled "The Poet in the Camp of the Russian Warriors," written in the memorable year 1812, did something to stimulate the national feelings, and procured for the poet a good appointment at court.[4]

It would be unjust to Zhukovski to ignore the elegance and finish of his verse: his only contemporary rival during the early part of his career was Batioushkov, who has much delicacy, but little force, and was not destined to fulfil the great expectations which his early productions had aroused. The unfortunate poet, quite at the opening of his career exhibited signs of insanity, and passed a great part of his life in an imbecile condition. Excluded from all intercourse with the outer world, he died in 1855. I may perhaps find here a convenient opportunity for saying a few words on the subject of Russian translations, and it must be acknowledged that few languages exhibit greater powers in the hands of a master. Hence the

[4] In 1878 a complete edition of the works of Zhukovski was published at St. Petersburg edited by M. Yefrimov.

Russians have long since familiarized themselves with the best products of foreign thought. Excellent translations exist of Shakespeare, Byron, Buckle, Mill, Macaulay, and many other English writers; and we cannot but feel gratified that, in spite of political antipathies, they have shown so great a passion for our literature.

The modern school of novelists—Gogol, Tourgheniev, Pisemski, Goncharov, and others, is formed, not upon Balzac and Alexandre Dumas, but upon Dickens, Thackeray, and George Eliot. Before leaving the subject of translations, mention must be made of that of Homer by Gnedich, formerly one of the assistants in the Imperial Library at St. Petersburg. This version is spirited and accurate, and the original metre is preserved. Some of the Russian critics, however, complain that too many archaic forms from Palæo-Slavonic are introduced, and that a rhetorical tone is communicated to the version alien to the straightforwardness and simplicity of Homer. To me it appears far superior to anything which we can show in our own language as a version of the same classic. If, however, only a translator was found in Zhukovski, in Alexander Pushkin the Russians were destined to find their greatest poet. His first work, "Rouslan and Lioudmila," was a tale of half-mythical times, in which the influence of Byron was clearly visible, but the author had never allowed himself to become a mere copyist. The same may be said of "The Prisoner of the Caucasus," in which Pushkin had an opportunity of describing the romantic scenery of that wild country, which was then entirely new ground. In the "Fountain of Bakchiserai" he chose an episode in the history of the Khans of the Crimea, which he has handled very poetically. The "Gipsies" is a wild oriental tale of passion and vengeance. The poet, who had been spending some time amid the steppes of Bessarabia, has left us wonderful pictures of the wandering tribes and their savage life. Many Russians consider the "Evgenii Oniegin" of Pushkin to be his best effort. It is a powerfully written love-story, full of sketches of modern life, interspersed with satire and pathos. One of the most interesting characters of the piece—we had almost said the chief character, but perhaps Oniegin himself must be considered the hero—Vladimir Lenski, is killed by his friend in a duel. The whole scene is put upon the canvas very vigorously, and it is not a little curious that Pushkin should have described so pathetically a fate which he was himself afterwards to undergo. He has shown true genius in his delineation of the character of the passionate and generous Tatiana, in contrast to her commonplace and conventional sister, Olga.

A criticism of Pushkin would necessarily be imperfect, which left out of all consideration his drama on the subject of "Boris Godunov." Here he has used Shakespeare as his model. Up to this time the traditions of the Russian stage—such as they were—were wholly French. The piece is undoubtedly very clever, and conceived with true dramatic power.

Since Pushkin's attempt, the historical drama based upon the English, has been very successfully cultivated. A fine trilogy has been composed by Count A. Tolstoi (whose premature death all Russia deplored), on the three subjects, "The Death of Ivan the Terrible" (1866), "The Tzar Feodor" (1868), and the "Tzar Boris," (1869).

There must always be a fascination to the dramaturge in this fateful epoch of Russian history, with its strange contrasts and terrible issues. There is a weird horror throughout the whole scenes of events, over which a Nemesis seems to brood as dark as that which directs the catastrophes of Atreus and Oedipus. Other authors have followed in the path so well opened up by Pushkin, and the Russians may boast of the existence of a national drama. The poet was mortally wounded in a duel, on the 27th of January, 1837, and expired two days afterwards in great agony. Such was the melancholy end of the man who has won the foremost place among Slavonic poets; Mickiewiez, the Pole, can alone be allowed to dispute the palm with him.

The Russian fabulists, whose name is legion, demand some mention; Khemnitzer, Dmitriev, Ivanov and others, have attempted this style of poetry; but the most celebrated of all is Ivan Krîlov (1768—1844). Many of his short sentences have become proverbs among the Russian people, like the couplets of Lafontaine among the French, and Butler's Hudibras among ourselves. His pictures of life and manners are most thoroughly national. In Koltzov the true voice of the people, which had before only expressed itself in the national ballads, was heard. The life of this sensitive and warm-hearted man of genius was clouded by poverty and suffering. He has, however, been fortunate in his biographer, the truly appreciative Russian critic Belinski, who has been accused by some of adding too many hues of romance to his account of the poet.[5] Koltzov was born at Vorónezh, chief town of the Government of that name, in 1809. His youth was spent in driving cattle about the steppes. At the age of sixteen he began to compose poetry, but he could not shape his fancies according to the strict rules of Russian prosody. At a small book-shop at Vorónezh, he purchased the works of Lomonósov, Derzhavin, and Bogdanóvich, and thereby became the master of the more artificial portion of his craft. Assisted by the son of a country gentleman, named Stankevich, he was enabled to publish a small volume of poems at Moscow, which became very popular. His life,

[5] See articles in "Drevnaia i Novaia Rossia" (Old and New Russia).

however, was on the whole a sad one; and during his latter years he endured much ill-treatment from members of his family. His letters give us a sad picture of Russian domestic life among the lower classes. Worn out in body and mind, the unfortunate poet died on the 19th of October, 1842.

The poems of Koltzov are written, for the most part, in an unrhymed verse; the sharp, well-defined accent in Russian amply satisfying the ear, as in German. His poetical taste had been nurtured by the popular lays of his country. He has caught their colouring as truly as Burns did that of the Scottish minstrelsy. He is unquestionably the most national poet that Russia has produced; Slepoushkin and Alipanov, two other peasant poets, who made some little noise in their time, cannot for one moment be compared with him: but on the other hand, he has been excelled by the fiery energy and picturesque power of the Cossack, Taras Shevchenko, of whom I shall speak shortly. Since the death of Pushkin, Lermontov alone has appeared to dispute the poetical crown with him. The short life of this author (1814-41) ended in the same way as Pushkin's —in a duel provoked by himself. Many of his lyrics are exquisite, and have become standard poems in Russia, such as the "Gifts of Terek" and "The Cradle Song of the Cossack Mother." In the piece entitled "Song about the Tzar Ivan Vasilievich, the Young Oprichnik, and the Bold Merchant Kalashnikov," Lermontov has imitated the old national Russian legends; we seem to be reading a veritable bîlina. His poems are characterized by a terrible vein of irony; the emptiness of life, "that stupid jest," as he calls it, is constantly paraded before us. Pushkin is also tinged with the same feeling, which seems to be something more than a note caught from Byron. Concerning Lermontov, I must mention a fact, interesting in our part of Europe; he was of Scotch descent, the original name being Learmont, and the termination merely added to Russify it. The poet has alluded to this fact in some verses, which have not been included in the ordinary editions of his poems, but were published a little time ago in the Russian Review "Starina." At what time the poet's ancestors settled in Russia we are unable to state; but any one consulting early documents will find many Carmichaels, Hamiltons, &c., in the time of Alexis Mikhailovich, to say nothing of Scotch soldiers in the pay of the False Demetrius. Every one has heard of the Bruces and Gordons of a later period. In Gogol, who died in 1852, the Russians had to lament the loss of a keen and vigorous satirist. With a happy humour reminding us of Dickens in his best moods, he has sketched all classes of society in the " Dead Souls," perhaps the cleverest of all Russian novels. No one, also, has reproduced the scenery and habits of Little Russia, of which he was a native, more vigorously than Gogol, whether in the pictures of country life in his " Old-fashioned Household " (if we may translate in so free a manner the title " Starovetskie Pomestchiki), or in the wilder sketches of the struggles which took place between the Poles and Cossacks in " Taras Boulba." The description of the Sech or Cossack Republic is drawn very vigorously, but the manners are too savage to render the piece interesting. The conclusion, in which the stern old fanatic, who has burnt to death many of his prisoners, himself meets with the same fate at the hands of his enemies, is absolutely revolting. For myself, the most charming bits in Gogol are the little quaint, humourous touches, as when he draws his picture of the sleepy old country-house, and tells us how each of the doors had a separate sound as it turned on its hinges, and an articulation for those who could comprehend it—just as Dickens put life in the bells in his "Chimes." In the "Portrait" and "Memoirs of a Madman," Gogol shows a weird power, which may be compared with that of the fantastic American, Edgar Allan Poe. Besides his novels, he wrote a brilliant comedy called the "Revisor," dealing with the evils of the bureaucracy.

Towards the end of the year 1877, died Nicholas, Nekrasov, the most remarkable poet produced by Russia since Lermontov. He has left six volumes of poetry, of a peculiarly realistic type, chiefly dwelling upon the misfortunes of the Russian peasantry, and putting before us most forcibly the dull grey tints of their monotonous and purposeless life. There is something of the spirit of Crabbe in these poems. A great concourse of people followed their favourite poet to his last resting-place.[6]

I have not space to enumerate here even the most prominent Russian novelists. No account, however, of their literature would be anything like complete which omitted the name of Ivan Tourgheniev, whose reputation is European. With the Russians, as I have previously said, the English novel of the realistic type, is the fashionable model. In this branch of literature, French influences have hardly been felt at all. The historical novel—an echo of the great romances of Sir Walter Scott—had its cultivators in such writers as Zagoskin and Lazhechnikov; but at the present time, with the exception of the recent productions Count Tolstoi, it is a form of literature as dead in Russia as in our own country. The novel of domestic life bids fair to swallow up all the rest, and it is to this that the Russians are devoting their attention.

Tourgheniev first made a name by his "Memoirs of a Sportsman," a powerfully written work, in which harrowing descriptions are given of the

[6] See Goloubev's Biographical and Critical Notice, St. Petersburg, 1878.

miserable condition of the Russian serfs. Since the publication of this novel, or rather series of sketches, he has written a succession of able works of the same kind, in which all classes of Russian society have been reviewed. No more pathetic tale than " the Gentleman's Retreat " (Dvorianskoe Gnezdo) can be shown in the literature of any country. There are touches in it worthy of George Eliot. In " Fathers and Children " and " Smoke," Tourgheniev has grappled with the nihilistic ideas which for a long time have been so current in Russia. The great novelist is still in the full vigour of his genius, and much more may be hoped from him.

The study of Russian history, so well commenced by Karamzin, has been further developed by Oustriálov and Solóviev. The former, who died in 1870, made some very important contributions to the literature of his country. His most celebrated production is his " History of Peter the Great," which was written with the help of many documents which had remained up to the time unpublished. The secret archives of Moscow and St. Petersburg were laid open to the author. The whole history of the unfortunate Alexis was narrated in the minutest details, and the circumstances of his fate made clear.

Last year (1879) saw the death of Sergius Solóviev, whose voluminous history had already reached its twenty-eighth volume.[7] Such a monumental work may well be styled a κτῆμα εἰς ἀεί; but it lacks symmetry and proportion, and seems likely to be rather a quarry of materials for future writers than anything else. At all events, it must be continually consulted by those who wish to treat of the great Slavonic Empire.

Before leaving this chapter, in which an attempt has been made to give the reader a slight sketch of Russian literature, about which but little is known in our own country, I will say a few words about the literatures of the dialects, which are at best but scanty.

The Malo-Russian is very rich in Skazki (national tales) and in songs. Peculiar to them is the Douma, a kind of narrative poem, in which

[7] Fragments of the 29th have been published. At the time of the author's death this great work had reached the earlier years of the reign of Catherine II.

the metre is generally very irregular; but a sort of rhythm is preserved by the recurrence of accentuated syllables. The douma of the Little Russians corresponds to the bilina of the Great Russians. In 1819 Prince Tzertelev gave the world a small volume of these under the title "Attempt at a Collection of Ancient Songs of Little Russia." Others followed, edited by Shpigotzki and Sreznevski and in 1834 there appeared at Moscow an octavo volume by Mikhail Maksimovich, in which a very interesting anthology of these curious poems was put forth, with explanations both historical and philological. These works, however, have been thrown into the shade by the elaborate edition, now in course of publication by Messrs. Antonovich and Dragomanov. On the national legends valuable works have been published by Koulish and Roudchenko.

Many of the Malo-Russian philologists, among others Koulish, are anxious to claim a higher position for their native idiom, taking their stand on the fact that Kiev in Little Russia, was the ancient capital of Slavonic civilization, in the good days of Vladimir and his heroes of the epic cycle; they vindicate for this dialect the right to be styled the Russian properly so-called. With them the Great Russian was only accidentally protruded from the fact that in the collision of the various Slavonic princes—one of the dreariest chapters in the national annals—Moscow came by mere luck to the front as the capital of the country. With this opinion, Miklosich agrees, and his decision must carry great weight, as being that of the most eminent Slavonic scholar of our day. Prof. Bodenstedt, the genial translator of Pushkin, who has admirably rendered many of the Little Russian songs into German, thus pronounces an opinion upon them,—

"In no country has the tree of popular poetry borne such lordly fruit, nowhere has the spirit of the people exhibited itself in so vigorous and truthful a way, as among the Little Russians. What a charming air of sadness, what a deep true human feeling, do those songs express, which the Cossack sings in a foreign country! What a tenderness, coupled with manly strength, breathes throughout his love-songs!"

As might naturally be expected, most Malo-Russian authors of eminence, have preferred using the

Great Russian, notably Gogol, who however, is very fond of introducing provincial expressions which require a glossary. Grebenko, however, and Kvetka, composed novels in their native idiom, and a celebrated writer of romances is still alive who uses the pseudonym of Nechoui.

The foundation of the Malo-Russian cultivated literature was laid by the travesty of the Eneid, by Kotliarevski, which enjoys great popularity among his countrymen. A truly national poet appeared in Taras Shevchenko, born a serf in the Government of Kiev, at the village of Kirilovka. He has himself described the vicissitudes of his early life. This highly interesting autobiography is printed in the Lemberg edition of the poet's works, and the new and complete one just issued at Prague, with details of Shevchenko, contributed by personal friends, among others Kostomaov and Tourgheniev. It also forms the basis of a sketch of the poet's life, appended to the translation of a few of his pieces by Obrist.[8] Besides poetry, the young serf devoted himself to art, with considerable success.

His childhood was spent in poverty and misery,

[8] See Taras Szewczenko, ein Kleinrussischer Dichter, etc., J. George Obrist, Czernovitz, 1870.

but his genius was awakened by the tales of the early days of the Ukraine which he heard from an old monk. How faithfully the poet has reproduced these interesting traditions, will be readily acknowledged by any one familiar with his writings, breathing all the spirit of that romantic part of Russia. Shortly before his death, at St. Petersburg, he composed some pathetic lines, in which he expressed his desire to be buried in his native Ukraine. The poet's wishes were faithfully carried out by his admirers. Near the city of Kanev, not far from Kiev, a huge tumulus has been erected in his honour, which not long ago was characterized by a writer in one of the Polish journals as the Mecca of the South Russian Revolutionists. Many of the poems of Shevchenko celebrate the early history of the Ukraine, the national heroes, Ivan Pidkova, Nalivaiko, Doroshenko and others. In the piece entitled "Haidamak," a fearful story is told. We have some graphic pictures of the battles between the Cossacks and their Polish persecutors, especially when the former rose against the Jews and Roman Catholics. The bloody banquet puts before us a ghastly picture, where we read of the murder of upwards of 1000 Jewish and Roman Catholic children at Human in 1770. The description of these atrocities is apt to become wearisome, but some compensation will be made by the fire and vigour of the lyrics of Shevchenko, who was certainly a true poet. Professor E. Partitzki of Lemberg has commenced an elaborate critique on his writings, of which a portion has appeared.

Shevchenko died in 1861, but the native bards of the Ukraine are by no means extinct. In 1874, appeared an account of the minstrel Ostap Veresai, and further details have since been given in the valuable journal, "Old and New Russia."

A good insight into the Little Russian literature was given by the Reading-Book of Alexander Barvinski, published at Lemberg in 1870. The first volume is devoted to oral literature, and gives extracts from the most celebrated songs, legends and tales. In the second specimens are inserted, among others, of the writings of Kotliarevski Kvetka, Gribenko and Shevchenko. In the third we are introduced (in the company of many others of minor note), to Marko Vovchok (a pseudonym of Madame Eugenia Markovich) whose tales descriptive of peasant-life have enjoyed very great popularity, and Youri Fedkovich, who employs a dialect of Bukovina. Fedkovich served as a soldier in the Austrian army during the war with the French under Napoleon III. Naturally we find his poems filled with descriptions of life in the camp. A collection of songs of Bukovina was published at Kiev by A. Lonachevski.

The Slavonians are becoming thoroughly awake to the beauties of their popular poetry. Of the literature of the White Russians, but little need be said, as it is very scanty, amounting only to a few collections of songs edited by Shein, Bezsonov and others.[9]

The subject of Russian Art has been very fully discussed in the valuable work of M. Viollet le Duc,[1] who must be acknowledged to be a great authority upon the subjects on which he writes. He finds fault with the Russians for abandoning their national style of art during the last two centuries, and copying servilely the models of the West.

---

[9] The periodical press in Russia numbered, in 1878, 400 newspapers and reviews. In 1877 the number of books published in the country was 7500.

[1] L'Art Russe, par E. Viollet-le-Duc.

He is inclined to see an Asiatic element different from that which prevailed in the Byzantine. At the end of the twelfth century Russian art, as shown in the ornamentation of manuscripts, &c. had reached a considerable development, but the portraits of the saints or icons showed a tendency to adopt a stereotyped form. This was to be expected to a certain extent, because among an uneducated people, religious teaching would be carried on a great deal by these icons, and M. Viollet le Duc thinks that the extremely ascetic appearance was given to the saints to inculcate among a barbarous people habits of self-denial and abstinence.

In Russian architecture, the author sees Hindoo, Persian, and other Asiatic signs; and especially mentions the church of St. Basil the Blessed, of which an account will be inserted in a subsequent chapter. In the throne of the Tzar Alexis, of a portion of which M. Viollet le Duc gives a representation, are traces of Indian work. In what way the Russians became acquainted with Eastern art has not been very clearly shown, but there was obviously a great communication between that country and Asia in the reigns of the earlier Tzars.

G

And, as M. Bouslaev, in his review of this work,[2] asserts, the influence of the Bulgarians, who attained so much importance under their Tzar, Simeon, must not be overlooked. One thing is certain, that in many of the forms of ornamentation among them the Eastern mind can be traced, especially in the interlacings of dragons and serpents in the initial letters of the manuscripts, the bulbous cupolas of the towers of the churches, and their positions in such buildings as the Kremlin.

According to the Russian author Snegîrev,[3] the different schools of icon-painting in Russia may be classed under four or perhaps five heads. These are as follows :— 1. The Byzantine, or Chersonian School. 2. The School of Moscow. 3. That of Novgorod. 4. That of Stroganovski. The first artists in Russia were of Greek origin, but they soon found Russian pupils. The models which had been received from Byzantium, were faithfully adhered to at first, but gradually the art of Icono-

[2] In the Kriticeskoe Obozrenje.
[3] Not having M. Snegirev's work at hand, I have cited him from the extract given by Mr. Bigg-Wither in a paper read before the Oxford Architectural and Historical Society.

graphy acquired a different character in each part of the country. It first developed itself at Moscow at the beginning of the fourteenth century, when the metropolitans were established there, having been driven away from Kiev by the Mongols. Peter, the first metropolitan of Moscow, was also the first painter of icons there. A certain Andrew Roublev, lived towards the end of the fourteenth century, whose productions were especially taken as models in the sixteenth century. With the beginning, however, of this century a change commences, as foreign artists were invited to Russia. They are called in the chroniclers Phriaski, which appears to signify "Franks," and nothing more. Their school was called by this name, and the head of it was a certain John Spissatello, who painted the frescoes of the Cathedral of the Assumption in Moscow.

With Peter the Great began the collection of pictures by great masters and ancient sculpture, which now adorn the capital of Russia. The Palace of the Hermitage, which is a continuation of the Winter Palace, is exceedingly rich in paintings, especially of the Flemish school. Peter laid the foundation of the Russian collection of sculpture by ordering the purchase at Rome of some ancient statues in 1718.

Since the great reforms introduced into Russia by Peter the Great, the Russians have shown an inclination to copy Western art—witness, the Kazan Cathedral, and other buildings at St. Petersburg. In modern times a few Russian painters have obtained notice, especially in the subject of landscapes, but no great artist can be said to have arisen. I must not, however, omit to mention Brioulov, who gained considerable reputation in the early days of the Emperor Nicholas.

Till the emancipation of the serfs the number of primary schools in Russia was very small; but after that event Sunday schools were opened, at first in Kiev; in 1862 they had already 20,000 pupils, when they were closed by order of the Government. After the Franco-German war, Normal schools were founded, but only in an insufficient number. According to statistics given by M. Reclus, the number of pupils at these schools in 1877 was only 4596, of whom 727 were girls. In 1876 the number of pupils in Russia formed only the eightieth part of the population. A certain amount of education is necessary for all the soldiers in the regimental schools. In the secondary establishments, gymnasiums, ecclesiastical seminaries, boarding-schools, &c., there were in 1877, 88,400 pupils, and besides these 41,630 young persons followed the courses of the special schools of the ministerial departments.

At the close of last century the institutions for daughters of the nobility were established, but were reserved entirely for young persons of that class.[4] But in 1857 a movement for the further development of female education commenced; and in 1876 there were in Russia 320 middle class schools for girls, with 55,620 pupils.

The Russian universities are nine in number— Moscow, St. Petersburg, Kiev, Kharkov, Kazan, Odessa, Warsaw, Dorpat, and Helsingfors. To this a tenth is about to be added, that of Tomsk, in Siberia, to which the present Count Stroganov has presented the valuable library of his late father. There is also talk of founding universities at Vorónezh and Tiflis.

[4] I have here continually made use of the facts accumulated in the volume of M. Reclus.

CHAPTER IV.

CHIEF CITIES AND THEIR CHARACTERISTICS.

In the present chapter I shall attempt some description of the chief towns of Russia. As a rule Russian towns are characterized by a uniformity amounting almost to monotony, very regularly-built streets, diversified with churches of the well-known Byzantine type, having five cupolas, and the bells suspended outside. The most exaggerated specimen of this kind of church is that of St. Basil at Moscow, of which I shall take occasion to speak shortly. It is said that the regular number of these cupolas was seven till the time of Peter the Great, who, among his other autocratic measures, limited them to five.

The town of St. Petersburg, founded, as everybody knows, by Peter the Great in 1703, is built on both banks of the Neva, and on several islands formed by this river, at some versts from its mouth. Fourteen rivers and streams and eight canals intersect the city in various parts. The usual width of the Neva is that of the Rhine at Cologne, and the Vistula at Warsaw; the water always appears clear and pure, and is delightful to the taste. This magnificent river is covered with ice from November to April. As soon as the thaw has set in, a cup of its water is presented to the Tzar, who rewards the bearer handsomely. As the severity of the winter is very great, so the summer is exceedingly hot; and nothing can be more beautiful than the long days at that season of the year, when even at midnight there is no darkness, and the sky assumes a pale green colour, so well described in Pushkin's charming little poem.[1]

The population of this city of palaces has been

[1] Luxurious city, poor city!
    Atmosphere of slavery, symmetrical prospect
    Under a sky of pale green—
    Weariness, cold, and granite.
See Pushkin's works, edition of 1859, vol. i., p. 377. Although there is no heading to the poem, its application is well known.

steadily on the increase. At the death of Peter the Great it amounted only to 75,000 inhabitants; at the commencement of the reign of Catherine II. it reached the number of 110,000; at the present time it amounts to 670,000.

The two chief streets are Nevski Prospekt and the great Morskoi. The city abounds with quays, made of granite (which is furnished in abundance by Finland), bridges, and squares. Especially to be noted are the square of St. Isaac, where are to be found the grandest buildings of the city, the Winter Palace, the Hermitage, containing a fine collection of pictures and curiosities, where the traveller will perhaps be especially interested with the objects formerly belonging to Peter the Great, his turning-lathe, &c. Nor must we forget to mention the collection of Scythian antiquities from the south of Russia, and especially the Crimea. The Senate, the Admiralty, the column of Alexander, a huge block of Finland Granite, the equestrian statue of Peter the Great, executed by Falconet, the French sculptor, and, lastly the cathedral of St. Isaac, in a modified Byzantine style. The interior of this church is especially gorgeous;

each of the pillars being of different coloured marble. It was commenced in the reign of Catherine II., but half completed in an unworthy manner by Paul, who seemed never so pleased as when discrediting and nullifying his mother's work.[2]

Another remarkable square is the Sennaia (lit. Hay-market) where the great market of the city is held. In the magnificent street of the Nevski Prospekt are found many handsome public buildings and private residences. The most noteworthy of these are the Cathedral of Kazan, the imperial palace of Anichkov, the public library with its magnificent collection of manuscripts and printed books, among the latter being the entire library of Voltaire, purchased at his death by the Empress Catherine, and the Gostinoi Dvor or public market.

St. Petersburg contains the statues of Barclay de Tolly and Kutuzov, the heroes of the year 1812, and also of Suvórov, the eccentric veteran who made the Russian name famous on many a well-

[2] Hence the epigram, the writer of which is said to have paid the penalty by exile to Siberia. "This church is a symbol of three reigns, granite, brick, and destruction."

fought field. His austere habits, fondness for practical jokes, and biting epigrams, were often discussed by our grandfathers, as any references to the newspapers and magazines published about the close of last century will show. He is buried in the church of the Ascension, at the Alexander-Nevski monastery. A well-worn stone, with coarsely cut Russian letters, bears the following short inscription, "Zdies lezhit Suvorov," "Here lies Suvórov."

Other fine buildings which may be enumerated in St. Petersburg are the Academy of Fine Arts, the University, and the Roumiantzov Museum. According to statistics, St. Petersburg is not a healthy city. The number of deaths is considerably in excess of the births, and it is only by immigration that the city is able to repair its losses. There is, however, a constant accession of the male population, no doubt consisting of young men who visit the metropolis to push their fortunes. All races of the empire contribute: most numerous after the Russians themselves, being the Finns and Germans. There are also many Tartars, who among other occupations are found as waiters in the hotels and restaurants. They may be easily distinguished by their dark eyes and hair, and short stature, so different from the blond type, and massive build of the regular Slav. One reason I have heard in Russia for these being so frequently employed in public buildings is their freedom from the vice of intoxication.

The suburbs of St. Petersburg are on the whole flat and uninteresting, but close by are the favourite Imperial residences of Peterhof, where many interesting relics of Peter the Great may be seen, especially his quaint collection of Dutch pictures, Oranienbaum, Tzarskoe Selo, and Gastchina, constantly inhabited by the eccentric Paul, during the reign of his mother. The small town of Cronstadt, strongly fortified on an island commanding the mouth of the Neva, has often been described.

The witty Italian, Algarotti, described St. Petersburg as the eye by which Russia looks upon Europe. If this city is altogether Western in appearance, Moscow may be accurately styled altogether eastern. The latter is said to have been built in 1147 by Prince George Dolgorukoi, the long-handed, and a strange legend is narrated about its foundation, but it was not a place of much significance till the time of Ivan Kalita (1328—1340). Through his agency the metropolitan came to reside at Moscow, and Kalita used all his efforts to give it the prestige of a great capital. Thus the spiritual pre-eminence among Russian cities passed from Kiev to Vladimir, and from Vladimir to Moscow. Kalita built some magnificent churches in the Kremlin, among others that of the Assumption, the Ouspenski Sobor.

The most important building of Moscow is the Kremlin, a triangular enclosure abutting on the Moskva, with strong walls, and containing thirty-two churches, of which the most celebrated are those of the Assumption and the Annunciation. Or it may perhaps be better described as an irregular polygon, with a tower at each of the angles, which is tall and surrounded by battlements. On account of the great historical celebrity of this building I shall perhaps be allowed to digress in a short account of it. It has been the great Palladium of Russia, and is regarded with almost superstitious veneration. Karamzin in his history has enumerated some of the most striking of these souvenirs. At the Kremlin Dmitri Douskoi unfurled his black flag when he set out on his expedition against Mamai, and Ivan Vasilievich trampled under foot the picture of the Khan, to which the grand dukes had been accustomed to pay homage. It was by the venerable gate of the Spaskoi, that Vasilii Shouiski entered, condemned to death, and was finally reprieved. The place is also shown here where the false Demetrius fell while leaping from one of the windows behind the palace. Within the walls of the Kremlin is included the arsenal (Orouzheinaia palata), a modern building containing a variety of precious objects which have belonged to previous Tzars of the country, among which I may mention the following. An ivory throne presented in 1473 to the Tzar Ivan III. by the ambassadors who accompanied the Princess Sophia, whom the Tzar had demanded in marriage, the cross of Vladimir Monomakh (date 1116), the original copy of the code of laws of Alexis Mikhailovich, commenced in 1648, written as is frequently the case with old Russian manuscripts upon rolls. There are many curious relics of Ivan the Terrible, among others an ivory comb and three ivory sticks and a small ivory cup belonging to Marina Mniszek, the wife of the false Demetrius. Several of these presents were sent by English sovereigns; thus there is a basin presented by James I. of England, in 1620. On the whole this may justly be pronounced one of the most interesting collections in Europe. Another building of importance is the palace of the Tzars, built in 1487 in the reign of the Grand Duke Ivan Vasilievich III. by the Italian architect Aleviso.

Here also is the Lobnoe Miesto, a species of tribune surrounded by a circular wall. As to the original employment of this place there is a disagreement. Some suppose that it was used for executions, others believe that it was the tribune from which the Tzars used formerly to harangue the people. The Cathedral of the Assumption (Ouspenski) was built on the site of an earlier building by the Tzar, Ivan III., who had invited to Russia the Italian architect Alberti Aristotile, otherwise called Ridolfo Fioraventi. The building was consecrated on the 12th of August, 1479. With the exception of the borrowing of some external ornaments from Lombard churches, nothing can be found in this edifice resembling the Italian style. It shows a greater likeness to Saxon and Norman architecture. In 1514 Vasilii Ivanovich caused it to be decorated inside with frescoes.

The Cathedral of St. Michael is interesting as the burial place of all the Russian Tzars till the time of Peter the Great, since whose days they have been interred in the fortress church of Petropavlovski at St. Petersburg. This building was erected by the Grand Duke Ivan Kalita, who was buried there in 1341, and rebuilt in 1507 in the reign of the Grand Duke Ivan III. by the Milanese architect Aleviso. Here among other graves may be seen that of the terrible Ivan, who forms the subject of many of the national poems. The following lines on his burial, from an old Russian song, are curious :—

Ah! thou bright moon ; father[3] moon,
Why dost thou not shine as of old time ?
Not as of old time, as before ?
Why art thou hidden by a dark cloud ?
It happened to us in holy Russia—
In holy Russia—in Moscow built of stone—
In Moscow built of stone, in the Golden Kremlin.

- - - - - - -

[3] Moon in Russian is masculine.

At the Ouspenski Cathedral
Of Michael the archangel
They beat upon the great bell—
They gave forth a sound over the whole damp mother earth.
All the princes—the boyars—came together,
All the warrior people assembled,
To pray to God in the Ouspenski Cathedral.
There was a new coffin made of cypress wood.
In the coffin lies the orthodox Tzar—
The orthodox Tzar, Ivan Vasilievich the Terrible.
At his head lies the life-giving cross;
By the cross lies his imperial crown;
At his feet lies his terrible sword;
Around the coffin burn the holy lights;
In front of the coffin stand all the priests and patriarchs.
They read, and pray, and repeat the valedictory to the dead,
To our orthodox Tzar—
Our Tzar Ivan Vasilievich the Terrible.

The Belfry of Ivan the Great (Ivan Velíki) was built to commemorate a terrible famine which raged in Russia, during the reign of the Tzar Boris Godunov. The original cross at the top was carried away by the French in their retreat from Moscow in 1812, but they were compelled to abandon it, and threw it into a lake from whence it was taken by the Russians. At the side of this belfry is another of greater size, which was built to contain the larger bells. It suffered greatly by the attempt of the French to blow up the Kremlin, but has since been repaired. It contains thirty-two bells, among which is the celebrated bell of Novgorod, which summoned the citizens of the Vech. Close by the belfry of Ivan Velíki, is the great bell which lies on the ground cracked, and is shown to all visitors. One of the strangest and most striking events in Moscow is to hear all these bells sounded at midnight on Easter Eve, as it has been well described by Clarke in his travels. "At midnight the great bell of the cathedral tolled. Its vibrations seemed to be the rolling of distant thunder, and they were instantly accompanied by the noise of all the small bells in Moscow. Every inhabitant was stirring, and the rattling of carriages in the streets was greater than at noonday. The whole city was in a blaze; lights were seen in all the windows, and innumerable torches in the streets. The tower of the cathedral was illuminated from its foundation to its cross. The same ceremony takes place in all the churches; and, what is truly surprising, considering their number, they are all equally crowded. We hastened to the cathedral; it was filled with a prodigious assembly, consisting of all ranks of both sexes, bearing lighted wax tapers, to be afterwards heaped as vows upon the different shrines. The walls, the ceilings, and every part of this building are covered by the pictures of saints and martyrs. In the moment of our arrival, the doors were shut, and on the outside appeared Plato, the archbishop, preceded by banners and torches, and followed by all his train of priests, with crucifixes and censers, who were making three times, in procession, the tour of the cathedral, chanting with loud voices; and glittering in sumptuous vestments bespangled with gold, silver, and precious stones. The snow had not melted so rapidly within the Kremlin as in the streets of the city: this magnificent procession was therefore constrained to move upon planks over the deep mud which surrounded the cathedral. After completing the third circuit, they all halted opposite the great doors, which were still closed; the archbishop with a censer then scattered incense against the doors and over the priests. Suddenly these doors were opened, and the effect was magnificent beyond description. The immense throng of spectators within, bearing innumerable tapers, formed two lines, through which the archbishop entered, advancing with his train to a throne near the centre. The profusion of lights in all parts of the cathedral, and, among others, of the enormous chandelier in the centre, the richness of the dresses, and the vastness of the assembly, filled us with astonishment."

It would be impossible for me with the limited space at my command, to enumerate even the principal churches at Moscow, but an account of this strange city would be incomplete which did not include that of the Church of the Protection of the Holy Virgin (Pokrovski Sobor) commonly called the Church of St. Basil the Blessed, near the Spasskoi gate in the Kitai-Gorod, which was built by order of the Tzar Ivan the Terrible, in 1554, to commemorate the taking of Kazan. It is of this building that the legend has been handed down, that the Tzar caused the eyes of the architect to be put out after he had finished it, in order that he should not build a similar one for anybody else. A more fantastic building than this curiously ornamented church, with its abundance of cupolas, cannot be imagined; it seems a fit memorial of the gloomy and grotesque tyrant by whose orders it was erected.

To increase the whimsical effect of its architecture, it is painted outside in glaring colours, and the interior is ornamented with a variety of frescoes. In 1784 it was restored by the orders of the Empress Catherine. The Red Square (Krasnoi plostchad) on which this church stands, forms one of the most striking views in Moscow.

In the neighbourhood of the city is the well-known monastery of the Troitza (Trinity). This is one of the most celebrated places in Russia, to which the pious are in the habit of making pilgrimages. The journey at one time was not so easy as it is now, since the railway has been constructed. Many villages are passed on the route. The wall of this large monastery is furnished with eight towers. The building was commenced in the year 1513, under the Grand Duke Basil, but was only finished in the reign of Ivan the Terrible, who in 1540 gave many valuable privileges to the monks to facilitate the erection of the building. The original wall was thrown down during the siege of the monastery by the Poles in the

VIEW OF THE MONASTERY OF THE TROITZA.

Page 100.

troublous years 1609 and 1610.[1] The most remarkable of the towers is that called Krasnaia (the red); it was built at the commencement of the reign of the Emperor Alexis. The new tower was finished in 1771 by the Archbishop Plato, of whom Clarke has left such agreeable recollections in his travels :—To enumerate all the churches grouped together in this monastery would be impossible here, a few points of general and antiquarian interest may be mentioned. The cathedral of the Troitza is built of white stone, and has its cupolas gilded; it contains some interesting ancient frescoes, which have been restored. Because it is built on the highest ground of all, this church is sometimes called the Makovka (summit). The Cathedral of the Assumption, situated in the middle of the monastery, has five cupolas and bears a great resemblance to the building of the same name at Moscow. It was built by Ivan the Terrible in 1585, who has left as great a name among the Russians as a church builder, as he has for acts of violence. This church contains the tomb of the

[1] The contemporary account of this, by Abraham Palitzin, forms one of the earliest monuments of Russian prose.

celebrated usurper, Boris Godunov, of whom it must be confessed, that although he obtained the Russian throne by violent means, his rule was on the whole beneficial for the country. Here also his wife and son Feodor are buried. Their bodies were transferred here by order of the Tzar, Basil Shouiski, from another monastery. His daughter Xenia, who forms the subject of one of the most interesting Russian national songs, was compelled by the False Demetrius to take the veil in 1622, under the name of Olga.

In a chapel near the Church of the Descent of the Holy Ghost, is the tomb of Maximus, the Greek, who fled to Russia when Constantinople was taken by the Turks, and brought many valuable Greek manuscripts with him. The cells of the monks inhabiting this large monastery are arranged in different buildings. Close by the Cathedral of the Trinity is an obelisk, on the four sides of which inscriptions are engraved, setting forth the services which this convent has rendered at different times to the state. It was erected at the expense of the Archbishop Plato. Besides the attack made upon this monastery by the Poles at the beginning of the seventeenth century, it is also interesting historically as having been the place of refuge of Peter the Great when young, from the violence of the Strelitzes.

At Moscow were born Pushkin, Lermontov, and Herzen, the socialist. A statue has, during the present year, been erected to the first of these. The population amounts to about 400,000.

After having described the most prominent buildings of the city of Moscow, I now turn to the third greatest city of the empire, Warsaw.

Warsaw, the capital of Poland, from the time of Sigismund III., to the extinction of the kingdom in 1795, is situated upon the left bank of the Vistula, which separates it from the suburb of Praga. It contains many handsome buildings, among others the royal palace, which was used as a place of meeting for the Diet, the Saxon Palace with a large garden, the mint, arsenal, &c. Near the gate of Cracow stands the gilded bronze statue of Sigismund III., whose reign was fraught with mischief to his ill-fated country. It possesses a university, where, however, since the last revolt, all the lectures and published transactions must be in Russian.

The university was founded in 1816, during the brief existence of the kingdom of Poland, under the constitution given by Alexander I. and it is only fair to state, as statistics show and Russian writers are fond of reminding us, that during this period the population of Warsaw increased greatly, and the trade of the city was very flourishing. After the insurrection of 1830 and the melancholy events which followed upon it, it was closed and not reopened as a university till 1869. According to the latest statistics, the commerce of Warsaw is in a very flourishing state, the city is full of distilleries, breweries, manufactories of tobacco, cloth, soap, and pianos—iron founderies, &c.[5] Lithuania and Poland both swarm with Jews, but especially are they to be found in Warsaw—the traveller from the west soon makes acquaintance with them, even at the railway stations, where they are conspicuous by their long coats and beards.

Vilno (in Polish Wilno) is situated on the river Vilya. In the early history of the Lithuanians it was a sacred place, and when Jagello, the prince,

[5] Reclus, 414.

became a Christian, on the site of the ancient altar he built a cathedral, which still remains, having, however, undergone frequent restorations. The population is very mixed, and there is abundance of Jews, as in so many other Polish towns. There is a remarkable museum, from which, however, some of the most interesting objects have been removed to St. Petersburg. The university, rendered so celebrated by the historian Lelewel and the poet Mickiewicz, was suppressed in 1832 after the Polish insurrection and the greater part of the books carried to St. Petersburg or given to the University of Kiev.

The cathedral is dedicated to St. Stanislaus, the story of whose martyrdom by Boleslas II. forms one of the quaint legends of Polish history.

The population is given at 243,512, of which a very large proportion consists of Jews. Close by is the chateau of Willanow, the favourite residence of John Sobieski, by whom it was constructed, many Turkish captives having been employed upon the works. The great hero lies buried at Cracow.

Kiev (47,424) although not the next city in order on the score of population, deserves prominent mention on account of the great historic interest which attaches to it. It lies on the right bank of the river Dnieper, and is the capital of the government of the same name. According to Nestor, St. Andrew the apostle preached here, and on the spot where he is reported to have fixed the cross, now stands the magnificent cathedral of St. Andrew Pervozvanni (first called). In 882 Oleg took Kiev from Askold and Dir (as the tradition goes), and made it the capital of his empire instead of Novgorod.

The most remarkable piece of antiquity to be seen here, is the Pestcherskaia Monastery, so called on account of the large catacombs connected with it, containing the preserved bodies of many saints, and among others of Nestor, the Russian annalist, alluded to in the chapter on literature. Besides this there is the Cathedral of St. Sophia, and the University of St. Vladimir, &c.

Kiev is one of the most picturesquely situated towns in the Russian Empire, and on account of its reputed sanctity it is a great place for pilgrimages. Both Great Russians and Little Russians visit the celebrated Lavra, or convent. Every year about

300,000 persons come to prostrate themselves before the tombs and pictures. The feelings with which it is regarded by Russians are well expressed in the pretty little poem by Ivan Kozlov, of which the following is an English version:[6]—

Oh Kiev! where religion ever seemeth
   To light existence in our native land,
Where, o'er Petcherskoi's dome, the bright cross gleameth,
   Like some fair star that still in heaven doth stand;
Where, like a golden sheet, around thee streameth
   Thy plain and meads, that far away expand;
And, by thy hoary wall, with ceaseless motion
Old Dnieper's foaming swell sweeps on to ocean.

How oft to thee in spirit have I panted,
   Oh, holy city! country of my heart;
How oft in visions have I gazed enchanted
   On thy fair towers—a sainted thing thou art—
By Lavra's walls, or Dnieper's waves, nor wanted
   A spell to draw me from this life apart.
In thee my country I behold victorious,
Holy and beautiful, and great and glorious.

The moon her soft ray on Petcherskoi poureth,
   Its domes are shining in the river's wave,
The soul the spirit of the past adoreth
   Where sleeps beneath thee many a holy grave.

---

[6] By T. B. Shaw, who died in Russia as teacher of English at one of the imperial lyceums.

Vladimir's shade above thee calmly soareth,
   Thy towers speak of the sainted and the brave ;
Afar I gaze, and, all in dreamy splendour,
Breathes of the past a spell sublime and tender.

There fought the warriors in the field of glory,
   Strong in the faith against their country's foe ;
And many a royal flower, yon palace hoary,
   In virgin loveliness hath seen to blow ;
And Bayan sang to them the battle story,
   And secret rapture in their breast did glow.
Hark! midnight sounds ; that brazen voice is dying,
A day to meet the vanish'd days is flying.

Where are the valiant, the resistless lances,
   The hands that were as lightning when they waved ?
Where are the beautiful, whose sunny glances
   Our fathers with such potency enslaved ?
Where is the bard whose song no more entrances ?
   Ah ! that deep bell has answer'd what I craved ;
And thou alone, by these grave walls, O river !
Murmurest the Dnieper still, and flow'st for ever.

Odessa was founded in the year 1792 by Catherine II. on the place were formerly stood a miserable little Tatar village. It is the next place of importance after St. Petersburg and Moscow on account of its commercial prosperity and advantageous position, but lacks their historical interest. By its population it is the fourth city in the Russian Empire. The inhabitants of St. Petersburg appear to the traveller to be of very mixed races, but this is still more the case with Odessa. The commerce is chiefly in the hands of Jews, Italians, Greeks, Germans, and French. A great many Roumanians and Bulgarians are also resident here. Till the foundation of the Bulgarian Principality it was a great centre of the literary activity among this people, as under the Turkish rule it was almost impossible to print any books in the native language. Here were brought and interred with great pomp the remains of the Patriarch Gregory, after he had been publicly hanged over the door of his own cathedral at Constantinople on Easter Sunday, April 22nd, 1821, by order of the Sultan Mahmoud. The exports from Odessa are chiefly cereals, wool, tallow and flax. Among other public buildings it contains a Botanical Garden, an Exchange, and an Italian opera. There is also a monument erected to the Duc de Richelieu, a French émigré, some time governor of the place, to whom much of its prosperity is owing.

This city, as will be remembered, was bombarded by the allied fleet in 1854.

Nizhni-Novgorod (Lower Novgorod), founded in 1222 at the conflux of the Oka and the Volga, a town of merely 30,710 inhabitants, but rendered celebrated by the great fair which is held there yearly during six weeks or two months. Its situation at the conflux of two chief rivers of Central Russia renders it well adapted for commerce. The fair, however, is said to be declining; it used to be visited by between 200,000 and 300,000 persons, Europeans and Asiatics. It has often been described by travellers. The chief historical event connected with Nizhni-Novgorod is that here in 1612 Minin, the patriotic butcher, and Prince Pozharski inaugurated the movement which led to the expulsion of the Poles, who had been harassing the country since the days of the False Demetrius. This celebrated passage in Russian history is often alluded to by the national poets, and forms the subject of a good novel by Zagoskin, entitled Youri Miloslavski.

Novgorod (the ancient) has now sadly fallen from its former prestige, and is reduced to a provincial town of 16.781 inhabitants; to pass it over, however, in this work, would be unpardonable, on account of its historical importance. There are very few antiquities to be found at the present time in this city, with the exception of the Kremlin, containing the Cathedral of St. Sophia. The town is divided into two parts, the Sophiiskaia and Torgovaia, which are connected by a good stone bridge. It was formerly one of the wealthiest towns belonging to the Hanseatic league, and the proud saying prevailed among its inhabitants, "Who can withstand God and Novgorod the Great?" It declined from the days of Ivan the Terrible, who treated the people with the greatest barbarity, and caused the bell which had summoned them to Vech, or National Assembly, to be carried off to Moscow.

Thus was destroyed the last of the three old Slavonic republics, Pskov, Viatka, and Novgorod.

Riga, on the right bank of the Western Dvina, about twelve versts from its mouth, is one of the most important towns of the Russian Empire for its trade. The population is 100,000. Riga was founded in the year 1200: it was acquired in the fourteenth century by the Livonian order of the sword-bearing knights; at the end of the sixteenth century, it fell under the power of the kings of Poland. In the beginning of the seventeenth cen-

PEASANT OF THE NEIGHBOURHOOD OF RIGA.

tury it was conquered by the Swedes, and after the year 1710, in consequence of the defeat of Charles

XII. at Poltava, it became a portion of the Russian Empire.

Revel is a military and commercial port, on the Gulf of Finland, strongly fortified. It contains the Church of St. Olaus, erected in the thirteenth century. Population 24,354.

Toula, a large manufacturing town on the river Oupa, contains a population of 56,679. This town is chiefly distinguished for its manufacture of arms, knives, inkstands, and all sorts of cutlery and works in polished steel. There are considerable iron-mines in the neighbourhood. Toula is of some historical importance, having frequently in the early periods suffered from the devastations of the Tartars. In 1610 it was one of the cities which rose against the Poles. By the erection, in the years 1638 and 1652, of the iron works, its present prosperity began.

Astrakhan is on the left bank of the Volga, chief seat of the government of the same name, and the only commercial port on the Caspian. The inhabitants are mostly occupied with catching fish in the Volga and the Caspian Sea. The eastern trade is a great deal in the hands of Asiatics. Many

I

historical events are connected with this city. In the year 1621, Marina, wife of the False Demetrius and Zaroutzki, the hetman of the Cossacks, took the town and delivered it over to plunder, and afterwards, in the year 1670, it suffered severely from the depredations of the Cossacks under Stenka Razin. The site of the present city is a little lower than that of the town of Atel or Balangiar, which belonged in the ninth and tenth centuries to the Khazars.

Sebastopol (or more accurately according to the Russian form Sevastopol) although sadly fallen from its ancient dignity, claims a short notice on account of its historical associations. Its magnificent bay has often been described; its importance appears, curiously enough, to have been first pointed out by an Englishman named Mackenzie in the Russian service.[7] About 1850 the population amounted to 40,000, but in 1854 it had sunk to 6000, its splendid docks having been destroyed and the city become, as Reclus says, a

[7] At the end of last century and the beginning of the present the Russian service swarmed with Englishmen, e. g., Greig, Dugdale, Billings—to say nothing of others.

vast ruin surrounded by cemeteries. It is, however, gradually resuming its ancient prosperity, and the "Malakov" and "Redan" have been turned into public promenades. In the neighbourhood of Sebastopol are many fine villas, Aloupka, Orianda, and the imperial palace of Livadia.

Bakchi-Sarai is an interesting Crimean town, because it has so completely kept its oriental aspect. This city was visited by Clarke at the beginning of the present century, and his description holds good at the present day. The situation of the place is very romantic, being situated in a valley between high mountains. It has been compared to Grenada, for it has also its Alhambra [8] in its palace of the former khans, with arabesque ornaments and abundance of fountains, discharging their cool waters upon the marble pavements. It is also surrounded by a large number of mosques, whose minarets add to the fascinating picture. The population of Bakchi-Sarai has also remained in harmony with its surroundings, consisting of Tartars, Greeks, and Karaite Jews, who are occupied as saddle-makers, jewellers, and gardeners. The circumstances of the

[8] Reclus, p. 836.

annexation of the Crimea to Russia have been previously alluded to.

An account of leading Russian cities would seem imperfect without the mention of any in Siberia, but it is obvious that these towns can contain but little to interest the traveller. They are, comparatively speaking, modern in origin, and the climate and associations are depressing.

Tobolsk lies on the right bank of the river Irtîsh, opposite to the mouths of the Tobol. The place was founded in the year 1587, but at first was merely a convict establishment, and was not called a city till the year 1643, on its restoration after a great fire. The place was in its most flourishing condition in the first quarter of the present century, but has lost its importance in consequence of the seat of government having been transferred to Omsk, and since the fair once held within its walls has been removed to Irbitsk.

The new port of Vladivostok (Lord of the East), with its magnificent harbour, promises to be a great centre of trade in Eastern Asia.

Without wishing to explain away or justify the severities which the Russian Government have

IRKUTSK, ON THE SIDE OF THE ANGARA.

Page 116.

exercised in Siberia, it will be well for the impartial reader to bear in mind the following facts :—

(1) The punishment of death is rarely inflicted in Russia. A large number of the persons deported, in most of the other European countries would have expiated their offences by public execution.

(2) Nearly all European countries, with the exception of England, punish treason and the higher forms of political offences with death—compare, for instance, the suppression of the Communists by the Versaillais; the shooting of the Austrian liberals Blum among others, by the triumphant imperialists; the executions of the Hungarians under Haynau, &c.—or incarceration for life in dungeons more or less noisome, as the Austrian Spielberg, and the Neapolitan prisons. For these Russia has substituted deportation to Siberia—a heavy sentence, it is true, but there are mitigated forms of it. The convict at least has the enjoyment of light and air; and the severity of his punishment is lessened by good conduct.

(3) At the meeting of the British Association at Swansea, during the present year, an interesting paper was read by the Rev. Henry Lansdell,

describing a journey in Siberia, undertaken with the objects of visiting prisons, hospitals, and charitable institutions. The opinions expressed by this gentleman must have greatly astonished many of the Russophobists. Let us also listen to a few extracts from an article in the Conservative Standard, entitled "The Future of Siberia," which appeared in November, 1879, and is triumphantly quoted by "O. K." in her interesting work "Russia and England, from 1876 to 1880" :[9]—

"The truth is, Siberia is a country of such extent that no general description can apply to all of it; and even when the accounts which have reached Europe have been true—which in the vast number of cases they were not, they related only to the northern parts of the territory. *Siberia is an infinitely richer and finer country than Canada, or the northern part of America generally.* . . . . . In Siberia the Russian peasant can get the 'black earth' soil, and he escapes, under certain conditions, the military service. Doubtless the 'unfortunates,' who are sent on an average at the rate of 13,000 per annum (or perhaps even as many as 20,000) to

[9] Page 219.

the penal colonies of Siberia, are not pampered to any alarming extent. But that they are nowadays treated with the severity they were in the times of Peter, Catherine, Paul, and even Nicholas, is entirely untrue. Indeed, since the accession of the present Tzar, who in early life visited the penal settlements, the bureaucrats' complaint is that so mild has the punishment of expatriation become that Siberia is losing its terrors. It is, indeed, the locality into which the Russian gaols are annually emptied, and an offender is sent to that country who would in any other be simply sent to a few years' imprisonment."

(4) That the surveillance cannot be so very strict is shown by the number of escapes. In Tomsk nearly 5000 exiles were missing out of 30,000. Not one third of the convicts sent for a limited time elect to return to their former homes, but end by becoming free settlers in the country. When some years ago, on a day of great public rejoicing, the present emperor remitted the sentences of several political exiles, many refused to leave Siberia. One case of a Pole I distinctly remember, who was making a fortune as proprietor of a flotilla of

steamers on the Amour. Let these undoubted facts be taken into consideration before we allow ourselves to be duped by slanders of Russophobist prints.

Tiflis. This is a very ancient city, having been the capital of the Georgian Kingdom since the year 493; owing to its exposed position, it has been frequently sacked; the last time being in the year 1795 by the Persian Shah, Aga Mohammed Khan. Of its old buildings only a few churches have been preserved, especially the Sion Cathedral, erected in the sixth century, and the church of St. David, built in the fourteenth century, in which rest the remains of Griboiédov, the Russian poet, who was murdered by the mob at Tcheran in 1829, whither he had been sent as ambassador to the Court of Persia.

CHAPTER V.

GOVERNMENT, POLITICAL LIFE, CHURCH, ETC.

RUSSIA is an absolute hereditary monarchy, for although Peter the Great by an oukaz gave the reigning sovereign the power of altering the succession, and thus paved the way for the *révolutions de palais* of the last century, yet the natural devolution to the eldest son was re-established by the Emperor Paul.

All power, legislative and executive, is invested absolutely in the Emperor. He must be a member of the Orthodox (pravoslavni) Greek church, of which he is the semi-sacerdotal head. The Patriarchate was abolished by Peter the Great, who regulated the relation of the sovereign to the church upon the protestant models, which he had seen in the west, and thus contributed to centralize all power in himself.[1] On Palm Sunday the

[1] See Reglement Ecclesiastique de Pierre le Grand, par le Rév. Père C. Tondini, Paris, 1874.

Emperor was accustomed to lead the ass upon which the Patriarch sat in great state. Peter was anxious to get rid of all this, and with a humorous touch of autocracy, set himself down in the Patriarch's chair, exclaiming, " I am the Patriarch !'

The Emperor is aided by a Privy Council, and in the general administation of affairs by four great councils, one of which, the Holy Synod, superintends the religious department, the second consists of the ministers,[2] and the two remaining ones entitled the Council of the Empire, and the Senate, exercise the highest deliberative and judicial functions. The provinces are superintended by governors, and the local affairs of parishes and districts by officers

---

[2] These are eleven in number,—
    1. The Imperial Household.
    2. Foreign Affairs.
    3. War.
    4. The Navy.
    5. The Interior.
    6. Public Instruction.
    7. Finance.
    8. Justice.
    9. Imperial Domains.
    10. Public Works.
    11. General Control.

elected by the residents of the villages, but of this I shall speak more at length presently. Finland, which was taken from Sweden in 1808 has, (as has been previously stated) a constitution of its own its parliament or senate meets at Helsingfors, and it has distinct military and naval forces.

The following are the chief Russian codifications of the laws.

1. The Rousskaia Pravda of Yaroslav, preserved in the chronicle of Novgorod, in which we see many of the same institutions existing among the early Slavs as in our own country, the trial by wager of battle, trial by ordeal, the circuit of judges, &c.

2. The laws of Ivan III.

3. The laws of Ivan IV., the Terrible.

4. The Ordinance (Oulozhenie) of the Tzar Alexis Mikhailovich, father of Peter the Great.

5. The great codification of the laws under Catherine II.

During the early part of the reign of the Emperor Alexander, especially from 1806 to 1812, while he was under the influence of Speranski, many wise reforms were introduced into the country. This able and generous-minded man was very anxious to carry out the emancipation of the Serfs, to constitute a middle class, and to give certain privileges to persons who had taken degrees at the Universities, but his plans were impeded by the violent actions of the secret societies which began to be formed and led, as is invariably the case, to reactionary measures. The persons who then gained the favour of the Emperor, were men of the stamp of Arakchéev and Novolsiltzov.

In order to abolish the foolish prejudices of the Mestnistchestvo, or custom which forbade a man to hold any office of an inferior grade to that which his father held, Feodor, the elder brother of Peter, destroyed the pedigrees and registers of ranks of the chief nobles, and ordered new books to be made, in which the names of the nobles should be inscribed. This paved the way for the institution of the Chin by Peter the Great. The word Chin, which signifies rank, is a classification of the civil, military, and religious dignitaries of the empire, and is as follows :—

1. Imperial Chancellor, corresponding in the army to field-marshal, and in the Church to the Metropolitan.

2. Actual Secret Councillor.

3. Secret Councillor, corresponding to a lieutenant-general in the army, and a bishop in the ecclesiastical ranks.

4. Actual Councillor of State.

5. Councillor of State.

6. Councillor of College.

7. Aulic Councillor.

8. Assessor of College.

9. Titulary Councillor.

10. Secretary of College.

11. Secretary of Government.

12. Registrar of Senate.

13. Registrar of College.

There are two kinds of nobility in Russia, hereditary and personal. The first is acquired by the rank of officer in the army, and by any position in the civil service down to the eighth class. Military officers on passing into the civil service with a rank inferior to the eighth class retain their rights as hereditary nobles.[3]

Children born before the promotion of their

---

[3] See " Russia under Nicholas the First," by Ivan Golovin, London, 1846.

father to hereditary nobility, are noble whenever the father acquires nobility by a rank or by an order. Personal nobility is attached, in the civil service, to the ranks below the eighth class, or it is conferred by a nomination of the emperor. Originally the Russian noble was exempt from the conscription; this, however, has been changed since the accession of the present emperor.

Each member of this grade is called a chinovnik; the venality of these government employés has frequently occupied the genius of Russian satirists, as in the "Revisor," and "Dead Souls," of Gogol, and especially the "Sketches of Provincial Life" of Prince Saltikov, published under the pseudonym of Stchedrin.[1] But the most interesting features in the Russian system of government are the Rousski Mir, and the Zemtsvo, which are so graphically described in the interesting book of Mr. Mackenzie Wallace, and which I shall proceed to explain.

The Rousski Mir (lit. Russian world) is based upon the communal tenure of land which the Slavs have inherited from their Aryan ancestors and still

---

[1] Of this book an English translation appeared in 1861, by Frederic Aston.

preserve. The attention of the English was called to this custom by the state of society they found existing in India, and it has since formed the subject of the valuable monograph of Sir Henry Maine, entitled "Village Communities." A more elaborate work, however, is now in course of publication by Professor Kovalevski, of the University of Moscow, who traces the remains of the custom throughout various parts of the world; among the Croatians and in the Cantons of Switzerland, to say nothing of the Celtic tenure and the so-called "lammas lands" among ourselves. In a Russian village, then, the arable and pasture lands are the property of the whole village commune, and the village is responsible for the entire sum which the commune has to pay annually into the Imperial Treasury. Each of these communes keeps a list of the male peasants, for the purpose of direct taxation. The government pays no attention to the number of persons who may be born between the times of the various revisions, till the new revision takes places.[5] Every peasant

[5] Those acquainted with Russian literature will remember how Gogol uses this circumstance as the ground-work of his "Dead Souls."

who pays these taxes is supposed to have a share of the communal land, and the amount of tax imposed has nothing to do with the quality or quantity of the land, but is entirely personal.

The Commune, says Mr. Mackenzie Wallace, has to pay into the Imperial treasury a fixed yearly sum, according to the number of its Revision Souls, and distributes the land among its members as it thinks fit. The revisions of the land take place about every fifteen years, and the land is then distributed according to the number of persons which the family contains. This would naturally occur after each census. But the various changes brought about in each commune by the deaths, the births, and the migrations, compel the villages to make the redistribution more frequently. In the same district, some communes divide their lands yearly, while others do not do so till the lapse of two or more years. The richest and best cultivated communes make redistribution of their land less frequently than poorer ones.[6]

[6] Reclus, v. 867, who gives as an example the survey of 278 communes in the Government of Saratov; those who make the yearly distribution are in the majority.

When the territory is vast, as in the northern provinces, the land is common to many villages, and constitutes a volost: thus in the district of Olonetz, about 600 villages are grouped in thirty communes. It is singular that even the German colonists on the banks of the Volga, although they received their lands in severalty, have united them under the communal system.

There may arise a difficulty, because the active members of various families would not be the same and accordingly, in some communes, an attempt has been made to distribute the land according to the working powers of the families; but the method of allotment depends entirely upon the will of the particular commune. The authority of the communal parliament is final and supreme. No peasant challenges it, and the Government never interferes.

The village parliament is presided over by the village elder, whose house is marked out conspicuously among the others, and who wears as a badge of office, a small medal suspended from his neck by a thin brass chain. The decisions of the communal parliament are generally made by acclamation, but whenever an ambiguity arises, it is settled in the Western fashion—by a division. The attempt of the Government about fifty years ago to introduce voting by ballot into these assemblies, resulted in a failure.

Communal land in Russia is of three kinds ; the land on which the village is built, the arable and the meadow land. On the first of these each possesses a house and garden which are their hereditary property, and not affected by the periodical distributions. I may remark by the way that the cottage (izba) of a Russian peasant is built entirely of wood, the beams being laid cross-wise, and the roof jutting out far beyond the bases. The furniture is of a scanty description, and in addition to the chairs and table, there is a large pech or stove, upon which the family sleep, and the sacred ikon in the corner of the room, with a lamp burning before it. The distribution of the meadow-land takes place annually. The division of this and the arable land is performed by the peasants themselves, who invariably effect it with great accuracy. In some communes the meadow is mown by all the peasants together and the hay afterwards distributed. The minor rules with regard to the time and manner of the cultivation of the land are all made subservient to the general advantage of the commune.[7]

A question will naturally arise here: How has the "mir" fared since the emancipation of the Serfs? It has stood its ground in a remarkable way, undoubtedly because it is thoroughly accommodated to the nature and habits of the Russian peasant. The law now allows the commune to be broken up into severalty, but instances of villages which have availed themselves of this permission are exceedingly rare. Cases are cited of communes which have been dissolved so that they might be reconstituted in a more advantageous manner, and others have extended themselves by incorporating other lands which they have purchased. Altogether the subject of this tribal tenure of land is a very curious one, and well worth the serious study of the Englishman, who is too apt to thrust his pet theories of primogeniture and private

---

[7] In my notice of the Commune I have used Mr. Mackenzie Wallace's work, since, although familiar with the Russian villages, I have not made a special study of the Communal tenure. Some valuable hints have been obtained from Professor Kovalevski.

proprietorship upon peoples whom he governs, as in the case of India, without entering into the question of their adaptability.

I now turn to make a few remarks on the Zemstvo. This is a kind of local administration intended to supplement the Mir. Its functions are to keep roads in repair, to elect justices of the peace, to look after primary education, and sanitary measures. It consists of an assembly of deputies, who meet at least once a year, and of a permanent executive bureau, elected by the assembly from among its members. Once every three years the deputies are elected in certain fixed proportions by the landed proprietors, the rural communes, and the municipal corporations.

Every province (guberniya), and each of the districts (ouyezdi), into which the provinces are subdivided, has such an assembly, and such a bureau.

It is difficult to see how, under these systems, with the progress of time, the Russians should not be developed into a constitutionally governed people.

In the " mir," however, the sacrifice of individual interest to the public advantage seems to cause a stagnation of enterprise, and to bring about that "stillness of ages," which is alluded to so forcibly by the poet Nekrasov, whose loss Russia has recently deplored.

> There is noise in the capitals, the orators thunder,
> The war of words rages;
> But there, in the depths of Russia,
> Is the silence of centuries,
> Only the wind gives no rest
> To the tops of the willows along the road,
> And, kissing mother earth,
> The ears in the illimitable cornfields
> Bend themselves in an arch.[8]

The management of ecclesiastical affairs in Russia is entrusted to the Holy Synod. The priesthood is divided into the white clergy, the parish priests, and the black clergy, the monks. The black or regular clergy live in the monasteries devoted to the practice of a holy life. There is only one order of them throughout the whole empire, the order of St. Basil. These monks wear a long black robe, and a large black hat; they allow their beards and hair to grow. They are divided, as in the case of the Roman Catholic monks, into two classes; the

[8] Stikhotorenia N. Nekrasova, vol. i. p. 209.

priests and the lay brothers; the former being concerned with the service of the altar, and with study, the latter with the household duties of the monastery.

These monks never eat meat, their ordinary food is fish, milk, eggs, and butter, and on fast days, vegetables only. They take vows of chastity, and are allowed by the crown forty roubles a head, since the time when Catherine II. took away the lands which were formerly attached to the convents. In consequence of this their numbers are comparatively small. The white or parochial clergy are compelled to be married, but cannot take a second wife should the first die. Owing to the poverty of the secular clergy (as also in the case of the regulars) they are obliged to depend a great deal upon the fees and presents which they receive from members of their congregation, and hence are eager guests at feasts, accompanying baptisms, marriages, and funerals.

Dissent, however, is as common in Russia as in our own country. To enumerate all the different sects would be impossible. I shall take the most important. Among these Raskolniki are the Staro-obriadtzi, i.e. those who follow the old ritual—

a very extensive body. In the reign of the Emperor Alexis, the Patriarch Nicon, having corrected in many places the Slavonic version of the Scriptures, a great number of the people looked upon the changes as deviations from the Word of God, and formed themselves into a separate body. They have since broken up into two sects, one of which style themselves Bezpopovtzi, lit. without priests.

Besides these are the Molokani, a very quiet set of fanatics, living chiefly in the south of Russia, who resemble our own quakers; the Pomortzi, so-called because dwelling on the shores of the White Sea; the Fedosievtzi, or followers of one Feodosii (Theodosius), a peasant, and Philipovtzi, the sect founded by another peasant named Philip—of very austere doctrines. Others are the Christian Strangers (Stranniki), and the Skoptzi, who mutilate themselves. The number of followers of the Old Ritualists and Bezpopovtzi is said to be not less than 7,000,000,[9] and the sects amount to 3,000,000. We shall thus see that in Russia there are 10,000,000

[9] See Mackenzie Wallace and the notes to the article Rouskii Raskol in "Old and New Russia," Dec. 1879, p. 523.

of dissenters from the Orthodox Church, exclusive of the Protestants, Roman Catholics, and Jews to be found in the empire.

The persecutions which these miserable fanatics have undergone at different periods of Russian history are indeed melancholy to contemplate. Many of them betaking themselves to the vast forests of the empire, led the lives of hermits or savages. Some burnt themselves to death, by a kind of voluntary *auto-da-fe*. Although active persecution has to all intents and purposes ceased, still the position of the Staro-obriadtzi is not an enviable one, and it is hoped that the present emperor will do something to alleviate it.

The Clergy in Russia are for the most part men of inferior education, and little raised above the condition of peasants. Still, no doubt, their vice and ignorance have been greatly exaggerated, to judge by such stories as Father Gagarin has taken the trouble to preserve. That the upper Clergy have been often men of high culture, we know, by the interesting account given by Clarke the traveller, of his interview with Plato, the Archbishop of Moscow, at the close of last century. Still there is a general feeling in Russia that the social status of the Clergy ought to be improved, and such an opinion was very vigorously expressed in a small work which appeared a few years ago, entitled " The Village Clergy " (Selskoe Doukhoventsvo).

As might be expected from the vast size of the empire, the votaries of many religions are to be found in Russia, and their several faiths are equally tolerated, whether Roman Catholics, Protestants, or Jews.

The Bishops in Russia are chosen by the Synod, but in reality are nominees of the emperor. The Church is divided into eparchies, the limits of which are almost always identical with the civil Governments. The number of ecclesiastics of all kinds in Russia is computed at 254,000 persons, of whom 70,000 officiate in the 625 cathedrals, the 39,400 churches, and the 13,000 chapels of the empire. There are 480 religious houses for men, but only 70 for women. A person who is prepared to find only barbarism and squalor in Russia, will be frequently surprised at the elegance and taste shown in the decorations of even remote village churches. He will also be greatly surprised at the number of beggars clustering about their gates, for the Russian laws concerning mendicity are very much behind those of the rest of Europe. A beggar with them is still regarded as almost a holy person, and it is a strange sight to see the large crowd of them surrounding the entrance of the great Cathedral of St. Isaac at St. Petersburg, and to hear the voluminousness of their pious vows and benedictions for the person who has given them an alms.

It would be impossible in a short work like the present to give anything like a description of the ceremonies of the Russo-Greek Church. Those who desire information upon the subjects may be referred to the "Rites and Customs of the Greco-Russian Church" (Rivingtons, 1868), by Madame Románov, an English lady married to a Russian. The style of the book is somewhat gossiping, but it is very readable.

The following table is given by Reclus, of the different religions of European Russia, in 1879:—

Orthodox Greeks and Raskolniks   63,835,000

Roman Catholics	8,300,000
Protestants	2,950,000
United Greeks (Uniates), and Armenians	55,000
Jews	3,000,000
Mahometans	2,000,000
Pagans and Buddhists	26,000

I shall now say a few words on the Russian Army and Navy.

Since the Franco-Prussian War the Russian army has been entirely reorganized. Previous to 1874 it was conscripted from peasants and workmen in towns, but since that time it has been reconstituted on the Prussian model. Every able-bodied man who has attained his twenty-first year is liable, and no substitutes are allowed. The regular period of service is fifteen years, six of which are spent in active service, and nine in the reserve.

The Russian army varies according to the time of peace or war, and oscillates between 710,000 to more than 1,200,000 men. On the 1st of January, 1877, Russia had more than a million men under arms, as follows,—

	Men.
Infantry	784,161
Cavalry	70,925
Artillery	125,927
Engineers	24,812
Total	1,005,825

The organization of the Cossacks is special; their mobilization takes place within ten days from the time when they are called out. On the 1st of January, 1877, the European Cossacks appeared in the field to the number of 40,000 men; their full complement would be upwards of 100,000.

The navy, according to the returns of 1878, was as follows:—

	Ironclads.	Steam-vessels.	Sailing-vessels.
Baltic Fleet	24	230	212
Black Sea Fleet	4	60	24
Caspian	—	16	9

Of railways, there were open on the 1st of January, 1879, 14,473 miles. There are 3678 post-offices, carrying in 1878, 92,692,540 letters. Of telegraphs, there are 2362 offices, with 68,000 miles of wire.[1]

[1] See Whitaker's Almanack, 1880.

CHAPTER VI.

AGRICULTURE AND COMMERCE, RESOURCES AND INDUSTRIES.

AGRICULTURE is the leading pursuit in Russia, but a great deal of the land is barren, and an antiquated system of husbandry is in vogue. Latterly, however, there has been a tendency to introduce the improved methods of cultivation practised in the West. The best parts of the country for agriculture are the Baltic Provinces, and the lands of the Ukraine. But these are only exceptions, since in the extreme north we get the tundras, or great marshy plains, which produce only moss. Finland consists of little more than lakes, rocks, and sand; around the head of the Caspian is a great tract of sandy desert, and a great deal of Siberia is one vast forest. In the Baltic provinces are produced good crops of wheat, potatoes, flax, and hemp, and in the Ukraine abundance of wheat, much of which is shipped to England, and tobacco and beet root. In the Crimea a kind of wine is produced, which attracted favourable notice at the London Exhibition of 1862. The ordinary beverages of the people are kvas, a kind of fermented barley, somewhat sour, but by no means disagreeable to the palate, and vodka, a coarse kind of corn brandy. Good beer, chiefly brewed at St. Petersburg, is to be had all over the empire at a very reasonable price. Vegetables are abundant, and the Russians have plenty at their tables, and are inordinately fond of small gherkins (agourtzi) which they eat with their tea. Good fruit is procured from the Crimea, Bessarabia and Georgia. There is abundance of live-stock in the country, and horses, cattle and sheep wander over the Steppes in vast herds.

The horses are small, but hardy, perhaps some of them may be the descendants of the same breed which Herodotus has alluded to in his account of Scythia. Bee-keeping, and the cultivation of the silk-worm are also branches of industry in some parts. The forests of European Russia occupy an area of 500,000,000 acres. The predominating trees are oak, lime, maple, and ash. If we divide Russia, according to the varieties of climate, into three divisions, we shall find the northern region deficient in grain, fruit, and vegetables, but abounding in animals, many of which are valuable on account of their skins; there is also plenty of fish. In the middle region we get different kinds of grain, hemp, flax, cattle, fish, bees, &c.; and in the southern division, (under which must be included the Ukraine, abounding in grain), are to be found fruits, cattle, &c.

In 1877 the exports of Russia amounted to 106,000,000*l*. Her trade is naturally two-fold. (1) The European, carried on through the ports in the Baltic and Black Sea, and in this direction her exports consist chiefly of different kinds of grain hemp, flax, tallow, hides, sail-cloth, timber, linseed, hemp-oil, potash, tar, tobacco, &c.; and in return from the European countries, she receives woollen cloths, wines, beer, sugar, silk, cotton, brandy, iron, ornamental goods, coffee, china, earthenware, &c.

(2) The Asiatic. Many of the goods exported have been originally obtained from other European

kingdoms; as, for example, some of those mentioned above. From the Asiatic kingdoms are imported silk, cotton, gold and silver in bars, cattle, horses, &c.

RUSSIAN MERCHANT.

Merchants in Russia are divided into guilds. The first is composed of those who have a capital of

50,000 roubles, the second of those who have 20,000, the third of the possessors of 8000.

The influence of Asiatic customs upon the Russians is shown in the tendency to establish bazaars in their large towns, called Gostinnoi Dvor (lit. the Strangers' Court). Here we see articles of all kinds heaped together, both of the East and West. In many of the large towns, fairs (Yarmarki—a word borrowed through the Polish from the German) are held. Every Sunday, in the square facing the Soukhareva Bashna (Tower of Soukharev) at Moscow, a market is held, in which all kinds of odds and ends and curiosities are sold. The traveller, visiting this ancient capital, will be much struck with the picturesque crowd to be seen on these occasions.

The great fair of Nizhni-Novgorod has already been alluded to.

In the Budget for 1879, 31,315,508*l.* are set down for the interest of the Russian national debt. It is to be regretted that, although so heavily burdened, Russia still engages in fresh wars.

The following statistics explain the financial and commercial condition of the country:—

Budget, 1879	£125,793,142
Total imports, 1877	64,500,000
Total exports, 1877	106,000,000
Imports from United Kingdom, 1878	9,458,729
Exports to United Kingdom, 1878	17,803,852

The principal industries of Russia—not including Poland and Finland—were in 1875,[2]—

	Establishments.	Workmen.	Value of Productions in roubles.
Cotton	833	164,000	100,000,000
Wool	634	88,500	56,000,000
Flax and hemp	402	35,600	13,000,000
Silk	121	9600	7,800,000
Paper	175	11,800	9,440,000
Metals	388	13,500	12,000,000
Chemical products	333	5,000	6,500,000
Leather	3297	17,620	29,250,000
Tallow	893	5,330	20,000,000
Machines	132	33,910	29,200,000
Glass	193	13,370	5,382,075

Industries liable to excise duties,—

Alcoholic, (1876) 3913 : Sugar, (1877) 261 factories, 95,871 workmen.

[2] Recl s, p. 875.

Principal Articles of Commerce,—

EXPORTATION (in 1876).

	Roubles.
Cereals	216,810,000
Flax and flax-seed	56,655,000
Wood	31,070,000
Wool	12,965,000
Cattle	11,805,000
Hemp	9,348,000

IMPORTATION.

	Roubles.
Ironmongery	77,617,000
Manufactured goods	47,783,000
Tea	52,971,000
Cotton	39,581,000
Beverages	19,484,000
Tobacco	19,400,000

Concerning the coal-mines of Russia, different opinions have been expressed; M. Reclus, takes a very favourable view. According to him, the South of Poland, Central Russia, and the region of the Donetz, have not been sufficiently explored. He does not hesitate to say that the area containing coal is greater than that of any other country in Europe.[3]

[3] Reclus, p. 870. See reference at p. 27.

CHAPTER VII.

SOCIAL LIFE AND NATIONAL CHARACTERISTICS.

At a time when so much of an abusive character is written about the Russians, I must ask my readers to dismiss any prejudices which they may have previously formed, and to endeavour to judge them fairly. Mr. Mackenzie Wallace, in his valuable work on Russia, has given us a graphic sketch of the sleepy Russian of the old school; full of good-humour and self-indulgence. In describing such a character he might also be translating from the clever description of Gogol in his Starosvetskie Pomestchiki, or Proprietors of the Olden Time.

In the "Historical Sketches and Tales" of M. Shubinski is an interesting account of a Russian seigneur, Basil Golovin, which gives us a wonderful picture of the life of the old nobility. The great luxury in which he lived, his parade in going from his native village to the capital, the reports given to him every morning by the head serfs, and his strange superstitions, such as having a noise made outside the house at night to keep the evil spirits off, are all drawn to the life. In this sketch we get the real old Russian, faithful to his Tzar, even to slavishness, superstitious, but at the same time to do him justice, with many characteristics of real piety, and fond of luxury and Asiatic magnificence. The pictures of the lives of the nobles given in Clarke's Travels, are vigorously drawn and faithful (for the time), but the book is disfigured by the inordinate Russophobia which possessed the author. Many of the boyars of the time of Catherine kept open house, and the servants in personal attendance upon them amounted to many hundreds. The women were in the main illiterate, though there was a certain superficial element of French education, especially during the latter part of the reign of the Empress Catherine, when the Gallomania raged in Russia, as it did in so many other countries of Europe. Probably, no stranger sight was ever witnessed than the Polish or Russian noble, trained in the rudest and simplest faith to the God of his fathers and his country, and living in an atmosphere of serfdom, and at the same time inoculated with the doctrines of Rousseau, Voltaire, and the *Encyclopédistes.* Such a character has been cleverly drawn by Pushkin in his epistle to Prince Yousoupov—

> Like an inquisitive Scythian
> Talking to an Athenian Sophist.

But in the midst of this artificial society many noble examples of feminine virtue might have been found. The Russians have produced their patient Griselda in the person of Natalia, the daughter of Count Sheremetiev, one of the favourites and co-adjutors of Peter the Great. At an early age she was betrothed to the unfortunate Prince Ivan Dolgoruki, to whom Peter II. was warmly attached. On the death of this prince, the Dolgorukis were sent in exile to Siberia; and Natalia, whose brothers were anxious that she should break off her alliance with a ruined family, persisted in marrying her betrothed, Ivan. In the very interesting memoirs which this noble-minded woman has left, which deserve well to find a place by the side of those of Lady Fanshawe and Mrs. Harrison, she thus naively writes :[1]—

"Just think what consolation or honourable advice would it be for me to marry him when he was in prosperity, and to refuse him when he was unfortunate ; but I had made up my mind, when I had given my heart to another, to live or die with him, and to allow no one else to have a share of my love ; I had no such custom as to love one person one day and another the next ; such is the fashion now-a-days (i.e. at the time she wrote these memoirs, just before her death in 1771), but I showed the world that I was constant in love. I was the companion of my husband in all his sufferings, and now I speak the very truth when I say that in the midst of my misfortunes, I never repented of my marriage, nor murmured against God."

In a short time her young husband was dragged from his gloomy place of exile at Berezov, and publicly executed at Novgorod. Her account of

[1] See Rousskii Arkhiv, vol. 5, p. 15, were they are printed in extenso.

the agony of their parting is most heart-rending, but would occupy too much space to be introduced here. After the death of the prince she still remained for a year and ten months with her two little sons in Siberia. In 1758 she became a nun under the name of Nectaria, and died in 1771. Perhaps, as a specimen of the luxurious courtier of the old Russian times, we could not choose a more fitting person than the celebrated Potemkin (pronounced Patioumkin) whose whole career was one of vice and luxury. The strangest stories are told of his outrageous extravagance and whimsicality, as for instance, that in his library he had several volumes of banknotes bound together. The splendours of the entertainment which he offered to the Empress Catherine surpassed the most gorgeous descriptions of the Arabian Nights. But what squalid barbarism was in close proximity to all this magnificence! We might well say, in the words of Juvenal,—

> Simplexne furor sestertia centum
> Perdere et horrenti tunicam non reddere servo.

The end of this "minion of fortune" was characteristic: his body at a comparatively early age was worn out. But he obstinately refused to have recourse to medicine, and pretended to overcome his ailments by the force of his constitution. He lived upon salt meats and raw turnips, and drank hot wines and spirits. He made an attempt to remove from Jassy, where he had been staying, to Ochákov, but he had scarcely travelled a few versts when he could no longer endure the motion of the carriage. He accordingly got out, and a carpet was spread for him at the foot of a tree, upon which he soon expired. Such was the end of a man who had long ruled Russia by his influence over the Empress.

A mad plutocrat of last century with the strangest touches of barbarism was Prokofii Demidov, the descendant of a blacksmith who had been enriched by Peter the Great on account of services which he had rendered him. Some of this man's freaks exceed belief: he appears before us as a kind of Brummell or Jack Mytton Tatarized. Owing to the want of intellectual stimulus the grandees were accustomed to amuse themselves with dwarfs and mountebanks. The ladies were lulled in their afternoon siestas by the long bîlini or skazki which their female serfs could recite *ad libitum*. M. Zabielin, in his very interesting work on the domestic life of the Russian tzars, has given us complete pictures of these old-fashioned days. Here and there in remote nooks of the empire men of the old school may be found, but the race is fast disappearing. The superstitious woman of the old Russian style has been drawn admirably and in the firmest lines by Gogol in his "Dead Souls," under the name of Madame Karabochka. The justice of the picture will be acknowledged by all who know the country. Who that has travelled in Russia has not noticed the pious old ladies vigorously crossing themselves in the truest orthodox fashion as soon as the train has begun to start? There is also the clever caricature of Nekrasov in the poem entitled "What the old woman thinks of when she can't sleep."[2]

In opposition to this type we have the man penetrated by modern European notions. With many remarkable exceptions, it must be confessed that

[2] Chto doumaet staroucha, kogda yei ne spitsa. Poems, vol. iii. p. 57.

there is a want of sincerity among the upper classes in Russia, which is but ill-disguised by the veneer of French politeness which has been superinduced. The charges also of venality frequently brought against them, seem to be only too well supported, and could be illustrated by many anecdotes told by persons familiar with the country.

On the other hand Russia has produced men of which any country might well be proud. Let us take such a noble-minded patriot as the late Youri Samárin, a man full of the truest instincts; or such a generous enthusiast as Nicholas Kiréev, the first Russian volunteer killed in Servia, in July, 1876. The sweeping charges which have been brought by western scribblers against the whole race are malignant calumnies. A healthy sign in the modern Russian is the taking a pride in the national language and literature; as long as the foolish mania for imitating foreigners, especially the French, prevailed, there was but little hope of the development of a vigorous individuality.

The modern Russian noble has, in most instances at the present time, abandoned the extreme superstition which was the characteristic of his ancestors.

If we wish to see the Russian nature in its true light, we must not take the nobility, who have been so greatly brought under Western influences, but the peasantry. These latter are not without their pleasing characteristics, being light-hearted, docile, and sturdy. Their bravery has been proved in many a well-fought field, and the annals of no country can show greater heroism than the Russian soldiers exhibited amid the horrors of the dreadful winter in the Shipka Pass.[3] The faults of the peasant are that he is given to drunkenness, and is servile; perhaps even graver ones may be found.

I have already attempted to describe a Russian cottage, and may now add a few words on the dress of the peasants. In winter a Russian Mouzhik generally wears a sheepskin with the fleece turned inside, with a pair of wide trousers thrust into boots reaching up to the knee; in summer he frequently discards the sheep-skin, and wears a kind of red shirt or smock frock fastened round the waist by a girdle. The dress of the women is usually very gaudy, and in the place of a bonnet, a handker-

[3] O. K. quotes in her book (p. 187) the testimony borne by Sir Henry Havelock to the virtues of the Russian soldier.

chief, frequently scarlet in colour, is pinned coquettishly on the head. Nurses may be seen wearing the graceful old Russian dress styled the Kakoshnik, consisting of a half-crescent fastened on the top of the head, from which falls a long veil. The unmarried girls wear their hair tied in a long braid, and the unfastening of this previous to marriage is constantly dwelt upon in the national songs. Hence too the well-known Russian proverb, "Long hair, short wit." (Volos dlinen, da oum korotok). For information on this point and many circumstances relating to the domestic life, see the interesting work of Mr. Ralston, "Russian Folk Songs."

He has described all the curious ceremonies of the betrothal, for which there would hardly be space in a short book like the present. Suffice it to say that the ceremonies are of a very minute and protracted character, the bride weeping among her companions that she is to leave her home, and paying farewell visits to her friends. There is also a great deal of expense on these occasions, to judge from the statement of Ribnikov, quoted by Mr. Ralston, that a peasant will frequently have to pay as much as 8*l.* 6*s.* of our money for his daughter's wedding, and that, too, in a country where the wages of a labourer are so miserably scanty. But not only are weddings conducted in a very expensive manner, we find customs of a similar character attending funerals. Here we come upon the traces of our pagan Aryan forefathers, the calling upon the dead, practised among the Romans—

   Amissos socios longo sermone requirunt,—

and the "wakes" lasting till quite recently among the Irish. The name for the funeral feast among the old Slavonians was trizna, and it was to a banquet of this description, according to the story of Nestor, that Olga summoned the Drevlians on the death of Igor, her husband, whose murder she was eager to avenge.[4] Not only is a feast held in Russia on the occasion of a death, but also on many other stated days, the dead and the ancestors of the village are commemorated. It is this festival held in honour of progenitors, and so deeply rooted a Slavonic institution, which forms the subject of the well-known poem of Mickiewicz, entitled Dziady.

[4] Nestor (as printed in Bielowski's Monumenta Poloniæ Historica, vol. i. p. 559).

The mode in which the family inform any of their friends or relations of the death of one of their household is very strange. They send a messenger or a letter, the intelligence being communicated in the following way :—

" Paul Alexandrovich (name of deceased) desires his compliments to you, and wishes you may live long "—by this he means that he has ceased to live himself. The hearers express their sorrow at the news, and crossing themselves add devoutly, " The kingdom of heaven be his." [5]

In fact the Russian peasant, as might be imagined, is surrounded with superstitions from his cradle to his grave. Each festival of the year has its strange rites and songs. The forest has its lieshie, or wood-demons, the rivers their vodiani, or water-sprites, and ronsalki, or Naiads. Not only is the popular poetry full of allusions to these mysterious beings, but the legends concerning them have been woven into some of the most graceful productions of Pushkin and Mickiewicz. A curious personage is the Domovoi, or house-spirit, who is represented as a

[5] Cf. Madame Románov, cited before, p. 138.

hairy dwarf, and said to have his habitation in the stove.[6]

As in our own country we have not yet got rid of the herb-doctor and the wise woman, we may

A DEALER IN ICE.

well believe that in Russia charms, incantations, and mystic remedies in the case of disease, are in full vogue. A considerable list of these, including

[6] Ralston, Songs of the Russian People, 119.

many which belong to the "pharmacopœia" of the "folk-medicine" of our country, will be found in the "Rites and Customs of the Greco-Russian Church," by Madame Romanov, page 227, a work containing many interesting details of peasant life in Russia, drawn from actual observation. In "The Legends of Old Time" (Rousskia Bilini) of Khanikov, previously quoted, are some curious remarks on this subject, with charms to cure toothache and other ailments. In fact, for a long time, a medical man was looked upon as a wizard in Russia, and among the peasantry there is still great disinclination to make use of his assistance. In the time of Ivan the Terrible foreign physicians first came to the country, one of the earliest being the Westphalian Doctor, Bomelius, who seems to have been a person of dubious morality, and like our own Dr. Forman, very useful in removing persons by poison, when his services were required. Having, however, been detected in a treasonable correspondence with Stephen Batory, King of Poland, he was put to death by his cruel master, after having endured the most terrible tortures, in the year 1569.

In 1581 an Englishman opened the first chemist's shop at Moscow. Since this time there has been an almost unbroken series of our countrymen practising in the country as surgeons and physicians. One of the most noteworthy of these was Dr. Collins, who was in the service of the Tzar Alexis, father of Peter the Great, and has left a very interesting account of the country, such as he found it.

One of the great characteristics of the Russian peasant is his propensity for song. And this, too, in spite of the harshness of his fate, especially so before the time of the Emperor Alexander II., the Tzar-Deliverer (Tzar Osvoboditel), who may be called, in the words of the Westminster Review, " the man who of all men of his age, of his own will and power, has benefited the greatest number of his fellow-men." [7]

By an oukaz in the year 1861, 22,000,000 serfs were manumitted.

Mr. Ralston has eloquently commented upon the songs which accompany the Russian peasant throughout his life. At different periods of the

[7] Westminster Review, January, 1880.

year set dances are in vogue, and the songs handed down, many of them from a very remote antiquity, refer to all the periods of a man and woman's life. Wedding songs (Svadebnia piesni) are very abundant. Many of them are variants of a stereotyped form, in which the bride is supposed to lament to her mother the approaching change in her fortunes: and conjugal life is dwelt upon as a sad change after the happy and exuberant liberty of maidenhood. The following, describing the arrival of the lover to carry off his bride, is pretty.

> Mother, a falcon [8] flies to our gates,
> Soudarina,[9] a bright falcon flies to our wooden gates.
> My child, my love, Nastasia, go to the court,
> My dear child, Mikhailovna, to the broad court,
> Mother, a falcon flies—he comes to the court,
> Soudarina, a bright falcon flies to the broad court.
> My child, my love Nastasia, go to thy chamber,
> My dear one, Mikhailovna, go to the dining-room.
> Mother, the falcon comes—he flies to the chamber,
> Soudarina, the bright falcon flies to the dining-room.

---

[8] In these ballads a lover is frequently called by the name of a falcon.
[9] Lady; the accent is on the second syllable.

My child, my love Nastasia, sit at the table,
My dear one, Mikhailovna, at the oaken table.
Mother, dear Fedor comes to the table,
Soudarina, Ivanovich sits at the oaken table.
My child, my love, Nastasia, bend thee lower,
My dear one, Mikhailovna, bend lower.
Mother, dear Fedor takes me by the hand,
Soudarina, he leads me from the table.
My child, my love, Nastasia : go thou to him,
My dear one, Mikhailovna, go thou to him.

The condition of the Russian peasant during the days of serfdom must frequently have been a very hard one. In some of the leading modern reviews, e. g. " Starina " (the " Antiquary," as near as one can translate it), and " Drevnaia i Novaia Rossia " ("Old and New Russia"), painful evidence has been given of this by the publication of many old government papers, and the recollections of elderly people. Thus there is the terrible story of the Saltîchikha, so-called by the people from a member of the Saltikov family, who murdered many of her female serfs, and was finally sentenced by the Empress Catherine to be immured for the rest of her life in a subterranean dungeon. Details have also been given of the cruelties practised by a

General Ismaelov, and the notorious Arakchéev, to his serfs. We are told of one lady who had been a great beauty in her day, and, being unwilling that the world should become too much informed about the decay of her charms, constituted one of her serfs her perruquier, and the unhappy man was kept in a kind of captivity, never being allowed to quit a certain room. He, however, at length succeeded in making his escape, and the whole story became known.

Gradually the idea of emancipating the serfs became a fixed principle of the government, but it was difficult to carry out such extensive measures, calculated to shake society to its foundations. It was certain that the smaller nobility would feel this great revolution even more than the greater, because the former employed their serfs so extensively as domestic servants. The Emperor Alexander I., a man of humane instincts, put an end to the disgraceful sales of these slaves by public auction, the announcements of which may be read in Old Russian newspapers, and form curious contributions to the social study of the period. I have already alluded to the fact that in many cases the peasant still clings to the communal tenure of land, instead of taking the share allotted to him by the government.

And here it may not be inappropriate, while speaking of the social condition of Russia, to say a few words on the spread of Nihilism, which has attained such a great development at the present time. The word is said to have been invented by the great novelist Tourgheniev. In order to discuss properly the modern revolutionary movement in Russia, we must go back to the career of Alexander Herzen, whom, however, it would be somewhat unfair to class among Nihilists, as he was a man of much more temperate character. Herzen was born at Moscow, 1812, the son of a Russian nobleman. He early developed a taste for socialistic theories, and was a great student of the writings of Hegel. Having inherited a large property from his father, he resolved to quit Russia, invested his money in foreign securities, and took up his permanent residence in the west of Europe.

In some most interesting papers, published in the "Polar Star," in Russian, under the title of

"The Past and My Thoughts" ("Byloe i Dumy"), he has given us vigorous sketches of the strange life which he led in intimate friendship with the leading political exiles, among others Kossuth and Orsini. The portion of the work on this country is especially interesting to Englishmen. It was in England that he founded the "Kolokol" (the "Bell"), a Russian paper of democratic principles. In a supplement entitled, "Under Judgment" (Pod Sond), minute details were given of cases of injustice and oppression on the part of the Government: these were ordinarily so accurate that it is impossible to doubt they must have been furnished by persons of high official position in Russia. It also circulated to a great extent in the country, but of course secretly. In spite of its democratic tone, it was always distinctly patriotic and Russian. An interesting account of a meeting with him and his companion, Nicholas Ogarev, is given in the "Recollections of Madame Passek," published in a recent number of "Old and New Russia."

In 1865 Herzen removed to Switzerland, and died in 1870. He was the author of a great many works besides conducting his journal—among them several novels; they were all interesting, and written with much spirit and verve, and it is difficult to arrive at any other conclusion than that Herzen was an honest man and a true patriot, who wished well to his country. Of a very different type was Michael Bakounin, who may be said in some sort to have been the founder of the Nihilists. He was born in 1814, of a wealthy Russian family, and early showed signs of insubordination. Thus, having been gazetted in the Imperial Russian Guards, at the age of twenty-two, he was forced to leave the military service. At Moscow he joined a club of intelligent men, who were great students of the philosophy of Hegel—among these were Herzen, Granovski, professor of history at the University of Moscow, and author of some valuable works, and Belinski, the genial critic, who has written such an interesting life of the poet Koltzov. Others were Youri Samarin, and Aksakov, conspicuous by their Panslavism. In the year 1841, Bakounin went to Berlin, that he might study the doctrines of Hegel more thoroughly. Afterwards he removed to Paris, and having refused to return at the command of the Russian Government, was now an exile. He afterwards mixed himself up with the affairs of the revolution at Dresden, was arrested, and sentenced to death; this sentence was, however, commuted into imprisonment for life. In 1851 he was surrendered to the Russian Government, and was imprisoned in the fortress of Petropavlovski, at St. Petersburg. His punishment was afterwards mitigated, by banishment to Eastern Siberia; thence he succeeded in making his escape in an American ship to Japan, and arrived in London in 1861.

Various accounts are given of the way in which he made his escape;. according to some it was effected in a very discreditable manner. On his arrival in London he joined Herzen, and became one of his collaborateurs in the "Kolokol," to which he communicated a much more rabid tone. In 1865 the office of the "Kolokol" was removed to Geneva, and here Bakounin plunged into the wildest socialism. He died in 1878, having been unceasing in his efforts to propagate Nihilism. One of his agents, Nechaev, had deluged Russia with political pamphlets of extreme views, and appears to have swindled the secret societies.

On the fraud being denounced by a Moscow student, Nechaev assassinated him, and fled to Switzerland, but was very rightly given up by the Swiss Government. Nechaev's trial brought to light the fact that Bakounin had filled Russia—especially influencing young half-educated persons—with political papers of the wildest and most rabid kind; he praised Karakasov, who attempted the Tzar's life in 1866, but deprecated further efforts at assassination, as the Tzar must be reserved for the judicial sentence of the people; the aim of the revolution was to be universal destruction; "absolute void must be created, for if one old social form were left, it would be an embryo out of which all the other old forms would renew themselves."[1]

At the present time there is a Russian socialistic press at Geneva, which is very active; many of its publications appear in the Little Russian language, especially the magazine entitled Gromada (The Commune).

During the last year the efforts of these misguided men have been redoubled, and have culminated in the attempted assassination of the Tzar in the

[1] Westminster Review, Jan. 1880, p. 173.

Winter Palace. Although these men were determined in spirit, yet their numbers would appear to be few, as far as it is possible to discover, and the movement seems confined to the upper classes, for as yet the deep reverence of the peasantry for their Tzar seems undisturbed.

CHAPTER VIII.

A SHORT SKETCH OF RUSSIAN HISTORY.

I HAVE thought it advisable in this chapter of my book to give some of the chief landmarks of Russian history. In this I shall follow the divisions given in his first volume by Oustrialov. He divides Russian history into two great parts, the ancient and modern.

1. Ancient history from the commencement of Russia to the time of Peter the Great (862—1689).

This first period is subdivided into (a) the foundation of Russia and the combination of the Slavonians into a political unity under the leadership of the Normans and by means of the Christian Faith under Vladimir and the legislation of Yaroslav.

According to the theory commonly received at

the present day, the foundation of the Russian Empire was laid by Rurik at Novgorod. The name Russian seems to be best explained as meaning "the seamen" from the Finnish name for the Swedes or Norsemen, Ruotsi,[1] which itself is a corruption of a Scandinavian word. It has been shown by Thomsen, that all the names mentioned in early Russian history admit of a Scandinavian explanation; thus Ingar becomes Igor, and Helga, Oleg. In a few generations the Scandinavian origin of the settlers was forgotten. The grandson of Rurik, Sviatoslav, has a purely Slavonic name.

Christianity was introduced into the country by Vladimir, and the first code of Russian laws was promulgated by Yaroslav, called Rousskaia Pravda, of which a transcript was found among the chronicles of Novgorod.

(b) Breaking up of Russia, under the system of appanages, into some confederate principalities, governed by the descendants of Rurik. This unfortunate disruption of the country paved the way

[1] See the Relations between Ancient Russia and Scandinavia, by Dr. Thomsen. Oxford, 1877.

for the invasion of the Mongols, whose domination lasted for nearly two centuries.

During their occupation the Russians were ingrafted with many oriental habits, which were only partially removed by Peter the Great, and in fact many of them have lasted till the present day. The influence of the Mongolians upon the national language has been greatly exaggerated, as the words introduced are confined almost entirely to articles of dress, money, &c. Had the conquests of the Mongols been permanent, Russia would have become definitely attached to Asia, to which its geographical position seems to assign it.

(c) Division of Russia into eastern and western, under the Mongolian yoke 1228—1328. This is a very dreary period of the national history.

(d) Formation in Eastern Russia of the Government of Moscow 1328—1462, which by the energy of its princes became the nucleus of the future empire; and in Western Russia of the principality of Lithuania, and its union with Poland 1320—1569.

(e) Consolidation of the Muscovite power under Ivan III., who married the daughter of the Greek Emperor, and succeeded in expelling the Tartars, and making himself master of their city Kazan. He was followed by his son Vasilii, who was succeeded by Ivan IV., who has gained a very unenviable reputation on account of his cruelties. Already the yoke of the Tatars had begun to have a very deteriorating effect upon the Russian character, and the more sanguinary code of the Asiatics had effaced the tradition of the laws of Yaroslav. Mutilation, flagellation, and the abundant use of the knout prevailed. The servile custom of chelobitye, or knocking the head on the ground, which was exacted from all subjects on entering the royal presence, was certainly of Tatar origin, as also the punishment inflicted upon refractory debtors, called the pravezh. They were beaten on the shins in a public square every day from eight to eleven o'clock, till the money was paid. The custom is fully described by Giles Fletcher and Olearius.[2] As the account of the latter is very quaint I will extract it. "He who pays not at his

---

[2] The Voyages and Travels of the Ambassadors sent by Frederick, Duke of Holstein, to the Great Duke of Muscovy and the King of Persia, fully rendered into English by John Davies of Kidwelly. London, 1662.

time mentioned in the bond is put into a sergeant's house having a certain further time to make satisfaction. If he fail, he is carried to prison, whence he is every day brought out to the place before the chancery, where the common executioner beats him upon the shin-bone, with a wand about the bigness of a man's little finger for a whole hour together. That done he is returned to prison, unless he can put in security to be forthcoming the next day at the same hour, to be treated in the same manner, till he hath made satisfaction. And this is executed with much rigour upon all sorts of persons, what condition or quality soever they be of, subjects or foreigners, men or women, priests or lay persons. 'Tis true, some present being made to the executioner, he suffers the debtor to put a thin iron plate within his boot to receive the blows; or it may be smites more gently. If the debtor have not to satisfie, he must be sold with his wife and children to the creditor." Another strange habit, savouring too much of this Tatar servitude, was that recorded by Peter Heylin in his " Little Description of the great World, Oxford, 1629," who says, " It is the custome over all Muscovie, that a maid in time of wooing sends to that suitor whom she chooseth for her husband such a whip curiously by herself wrought, in token of her subjection unto him." A Russian writer also tells us that it was usual for the husband on the wedding day to give his bride a gentle stroke over the shoulders with his whip, to show his power over her.[3] Herberstein's story of the German Jordan and his Russian wife will perhaps occur to some of my readers. She complained to her husband that he did not love her; but upon his expressing surprise at the doubt, she gave as her reason that he had never beaten her! Indeed the position of a woman in Russia till the time of Peter was a very melancholy one. Her place in society is accurately marked out in the Domostroi, or regulations for governing one's household, written in the time of Ivan the Terrible. As this book presents us with some very curious pictures of Russian family life in the olden time, a few words may be permitted describing its contents. It was written by the monk Sylvester, who was one of the chief counsellors of Ivan, and at one

[3] Khanikov.

time in great favour with him, but afterwards fell into disgrace and was banished by the capricious tyrant to the Solovetzki monastery, where he died. The work was primarily addressed by the worthy priest to his son Anthemus and his daughter-in-law Pelagia, but as the bulk of it was of a general character it soon became used in all households. Nothing escapes this father of the church from the duties of religion down to the minor details of the kitchen and the mysteries of cookery. The wife is constantly recommended to practise humility, in a way which would probably be repulsive to many of our modern ladies. Her industry in weaving and making clothes among her domestics is very carefully dwelt upon. She lived in a kind of oriental seclusion, and saw no one except her nearest relatives. The bridegroom knew nothing of his bride, she was only allowed to be seen a few times before marriage by his female relatives, and on these occasions all kinds of tricks were played. A stool was placed under her feet that she might seem taller, or a handsome female attendant, or a better-looking sister were substituted. "Nowhere," says Kotoshikhin, the author of the interesting book on Russia previously cited, "is there such trickery practised with reference to brides as at Moscow." The innovations of Peter the Great broke through the oriental seclusion of the terem, as the women's apartments were called. During the minority of Ivan IV. the regency was committed to the care of his mother Elena, and was at best but a stormy period. When Ivan came to the throne the country was not even yet free from the incursions of the Tatars. In Hakluyt's voyages we have a curious account of one of these devastations in a "letter of Richard Vscombe to M. Henrie Lane, touching the burning of the city of Mosco by the Crimme Tartar, written the 5th day of August, 1571."

"The Mosco is burnt every sticke by the Crimme, the 24th day of May last, and an innumerable number of people; and in the English house was smothered Thomas Southam, Tosild, Waverley, Green's wife and children, two children of Rafe, and more to the number of twenty-five persons were stifeled in oure beere seller, and yet in the same seller was Rafe, his wife, John Browne, and John Clarke preserved, which was wonderfull. And there went to that seller Master Glover and Master Rowley also; but because the heat was so great they came foorth againe with much perrill, so that a boy at their heeles was taken with the fire, yet they escaped blindfold into another seller, and there as God's will was they were preserved. The emperor fled out of the field, and many of his people were carried away by the Crimme Tartar. And so with exceeding much spoile and infinite prisoners, they returned home againe. What with the Crimme on the one side and his crueltie on the other, he hath but few people left." (Hakluyt, i. 402).

It is well known that the English first became acquainted with Russia in the time of Ivan the Terrible. In the reign of Edward VI. a voyage was undertaken by Sir Hugh Willoughby and Richard Chancellor, who attempted to reach Russia by way of the North Sea. Willoughby and his crew were unfortunately lost, but Chancellor succeeded in reaching Moscow, and showing his letters to the Tzar, in reply to which an alliance was concluded and an ambassador soon afterwards visited the English court. In spite of his brutal tyrannies, for which no apologies can be offered, although some of the Russian authorities have attempted to gloss them over, the reign of Ivan was distinctly progressive for Russia. The introduction of the printing-press, the conquest of Siberia, the development of commerce, were all in advance of what had been done by his predecessors.[4] He also had the leading idea afterwards fully carried out by Peter the Great of extending the dominions on the north, and ensuring a footing on the Baltic.

The relations of Ivan with England are fully described in the very interesting diary of Sir Jerome Horsey, the ambassador from this country, the manuscript of which is preserved in the British Museum.[5] He was anxious to have an English wife, and Elizabeth selected one for him, Lady Mary Hastings, but when the bride elect had been made acquainted with the circumstance that Ivan had been married several times before, and was a

---

[4] See the curious letter preserved among the Harleian MSS. in which Ivan asks Elizabeth to send him apothecaries, surgeons, architects, and other useful men.

[5] It has been edited by Mr. E. A. Bond, the present chief librarian.

most truculent and blood-thirsty sovereign, she entreated her father with many tears not to send her to such a man.

The character given of Ivan by Horsey is very graphic, and is valuable as the narration of a person who had frequently been in intimate relations with the Tzar. We give it in the original spelling :—

"Thus much to conclude with this Emperor Ivan Vasiliwich. He was a goodlie man of person and presence, well favored, high forehead, shrill voice, a right Sithian, full of readie wisdom, cruell, bloudye, merciless; his own experience mannaged by direction both his state and commonwealth affares; was sumptuously intomed in Michell Archangell Church, where he, though garded daye and night, remaines a fearfull spectacle to the memorie of such as pass by or heer his name spoken of [who] are contented to cross and bless themselves from his resurrection againe."

Passing over his feeble son, we come to the era of Boris Godunov, a man in many respects remarkable, but not the least that he saw the necessity of western culture. His plans for educating

Russia were extensive, and several youths were sent abroad for this purpose, including some to England. But his reign ended gloomily, and was followed by the period of the Pretenders (Samozvantzi), during which Russia was rent by opposing factions; and almost ended in receiving a foreign sovereign, in the person of Ladislaus (Wladyslaw), the son of Sigismund III., the king of Poland. The Romanovs finally ascended the throne in the person of Michael in 1613. The son of Michael, Alexis, was a thoroughly reforming sovereign, and took many foreigners into his pay.[6] With the reign of Ivan V., son of Alexis, closes the old period of Russian history.

One of the most interesting sources of our knowledge of the Tzars, from Ivan the Terrible to Shouiski, is the quaint chronograph, as he styles it, of Sergius Koubasov, who has left us sketches of the personal appearance of many of them, either gathered from his own observation or the accounts of eye-witnesses. Extracts from this interesting work

[6] See the extract published in the Russian Review (Starina) including the permission given by Alexis for the terrible Dalzell to leave his service.

are given by Bouslaev. Koubasov lived in the early part of the seventeenth century. As we prize his work, so on the other hand we must regret that the chronicle of Prince Mstislavski, which he showed to Horsey, according to the diary of the latter, and which contained his account of contemporary events, has been lost.

II. The new history, from the days of Peter the Great to the present time.

The reforms introduced into Russia by Peter the Great, are too well known to need recapitulation here. There will be always many different opinions about this wonderful man. Some have not hesitated to say that he "knouted" Russia into civilization; others can see traces of the hero mixed with much clay. One of the darkest pages in the annals of his reign, is that upon which is written the fate of his unfortunate son, Alexis. All Russia seems but one vast monument of his genius. He gave her six new provinces, a footing upon two seas, a regular army trained on the European system, a large fleet, an admiralty, and a naval academy; besides these, some educational establishments, a gallery of painting and sculpture, and a public library. Nothing escaped his notice, even to such minutiæ as the alteration of the Russian letters to make them more adapted to printing, and changing the dress of his subjects so as to be more in conformity with European costume. All this interference savoured of despotism, no doubt, but it led to the consolidation of a great nationality. The Russians belong to the European family, and must of necessity return to fulfil their destiny, although they had been temporarily diverted by their bondage under the Mongols. Owing to the mistake Peter had committed in allowing the succession to be changed at the will of the ruling sovereign, the country was for some time after his death in the hands of Russian and German adventurers.

On the death of Peter he was succeeded by his wife Catherine, an amiable but illiterate woman, who was wholly under the influence of Menshikov, one of Peter's chief favourites. After a short reign of two years she was succeeded by Peter II., son of the unfortunate Alexis, in whose time Menshikov and his family were banished to Berezov in Siberia, the dreary spot of which mention has been made in the early part of this volume. After his banishment, Peter, who was a weak prince, and showed every inclination to undo his grandfather's work, fell under the influence of the Dolgoroukis.

There is something very touching in the fate of this poor child—he was but fifteen years of age when he died—tossed about amidst the opposing factions of the intriguing courtiers, each of whom cared nothing for the good of the country, but only how to find the readiest means to supplant his rival. The last words of the boy as he lay on his deathbed were, "Get ready the sledge! I want to go to my sister!" alluding to the Princess Natalia, the other child of Alexis who had died three years previously.

On his death Anne, Duchess of Courland, and daughter of Ivan, the elder brother of Peter, was called to the throne. After her death, by a second *révolution de palais*, Elizabeth, the daughter of Peter the Great, was made sovereign. In this reign an alliance was concluded with Maria Theresa of Austria, and during the seven years' war, a large Russian force invaded Prussia; another took Berlin in 1760.

During the whole of her reign Elizabeth was under the influence of favourites, or *vremenstchiki*, as the Russians call them. She appears to have been an indolent, good-tempered woman, and exceedingly superstitious. During her reign Russia made considerable progress in literature and culture. A national theatre, of which there had been a few germs even at so early a period as the youth of Peter the Great, was thoroughly developed, and at Yaroslavl, Volkov, the son of a merchant, earned such a reputation as an actor, that he was summoned to St. Petersburg by Elizabeth, who took him under her patronage. Dramatists now sprang up on every side, but at first were merely translators of Corneille, Racine, and Molière. The Russian arms were successful during her reign, and the capture of Berlin in 1760, had a great effect upon European politics. Two years afterwards Elizabeth died, and her nephew Peter III.[7] succeeded, who admired Frederick the Great, and at once made peace with him.

This unfortunate man, however, only reigned

[7] Peter was the son of Anne, daughter of Peter the Great and Charles Frederick, Duke of Holstein Gottorp.

six months, having been dethroned and put to death by order of his wife, who became Empress of Russia under the title of Catherine II. However unjustifiable the means may have been by which Catherine became possessed of the throne, and in mere justice to her we must remember that she had been brutally treated by her husband, and was in hourly expectation of being immured for life in a dungeon by his orders, she exercised her power to the advantage of the country.

In 1770, a Russian fleet appeared for the first time in the Mediterranean, and the Turkish navy was destroyed at Chesme. By the treaty of Kutchuk Kainardji (1774), Turkey was obliged to recognize the independence of the Crimea, and cede to Russia a considerable amount of territory. In 1783 Russia gained the Crimea, and in 1795, by the last partition of Poland, a very large portion of that country.

The subsequent events of the history are well known. Paul, who succeeded Catherine, was assassinated in 1801. The reign of this emperor has been made very familiar to Englishmen by the highly coloured portrait given by the traveller

Clarke, who laboured under the most aggravated Russophobia. That Paul did many cruel and capricious things does not admit of a doubt, but he was capable of generous feelings, and sometimes surprised people as much by his liberality as by his despotic conduct. Thus he set Kosciusko at liberty as soon as he had ascended the throne; and there was a fine revenge in his compelling Orlov to follow the coffins of Peter and Catherine, when by his order they were buried together in the Petropavlovski church. An interesting account of this ceremony is given in the memoirs of Admiral Shishkov, who was an eye-witness.[8] Paul had ordered the body of his father to be exhumed in the Nevski monastery. On the coffin being opened, it is said that nothing was found but a few bones and the emperor's boots.

Alexander I. his son, added Finland to the Russian empire, and saw his country invaded by Napoleon in 1812. The horrors of this campaign have been well described by Segur, Wilson, and Labaume. Some very interesting papers, narrating

[8] See his memoirs (Zapiski), edited by the late Youri Samárin. Berlin, 1870; vol. ii. p. 14.

the sufferings of the Russians during the occupation of the French, have appeared in the "Rousski Arkhiv," the valuable historical journal to which I have previously alluded, edited by M. Bartenev. At his death in 1825, his brother Nicholas succeeded, not without opposition, which led to bloodshed and the execution of the five Dekabrists (conspirators of December). The schemes of these men were impracticable ; so little did the common people understand the very rudiments of liberalism, that, when the soldiers were ordered to shout for Konstitoutzia (the constitution, a word the foreign appearance of which shows how alien it was to the national spirit), one of them naively asked, if that was the name of the wife of the Grand Duke Constantine.

The policy of the Emperor Nicholas was one of complete isolation of the country, and the prevention of his subjects as much as possible from holding intercourse with the rest of Europe, hence permission to travel was but sparingly given, nor were foreigners encouraged to visit Russia. In 1826, war broke out with Persia, the result of which was that the latter power was compelled to cede

Erivan and the country as far as the Araxes (or Aras). Russia also made further additions to her territory by the treaty of Adrianople in 1829, after Diebich had crossed the Balkans. In 1830 the great Polish rebellion broke out, which was crushed after much bloodshed in Sept. 1831, by the capture of Warsaw. In 1849, the Russians assisted Austria in crushing the revolt of her Hungarian subjects. In 1853 broke out the Crimean War, the details of which are so well known as to require no enumeration. Peace was concluded between Russia and the Allies, after the death of the Emperor Nicholas in 1855, who was succeeded by his son Alexander II. The two great events of the reign of this monarch have been the emancipation of the serfs in 1861, by which 22,000,000 received their liberty, and the war with Turkey just concluded.

CHAPTER IX.

POLISH HISTORY.

As so large a part of the original Kingdom of Poland belongs to Russia, and its history is so mixed up with that of the latter country, I think it advisable to give a few outlines of this subject.

The early history of Poland is little better than a collection of myths, into the texture of which many old Aryan legends have been inwoven, such as the stories of the good peasant Piast, with which we may compare the Mikoula Selianinovich of the Russians, and probably the account of Cincinnatus in Roman history, rests upon no surer basis. With the reign of Mieczyslaw I. (962—992) something more certain begins. He turned Christian, and proceeded to extirpate the idols of his countrymen in the same high-handed manner as had been done by Vladimir at Kiev. At the commencement of the eleventh century, Boleslaw the Great had absorbed nearly all the Western Slavonic states, including Bohemia. But hostile elements were getting introduced among their numbers by degrees. Conrad, Duke of Masovia, and brother of Leszek, surnamed the White, introduced the order of Teutonic Knights into the territories on the Baltic, from whom the Prussian monarchy, one of the great enemies of Poland, was afterwards to develope itself.

At an early stage in the history of the country, the Germans and Jews entered it. The natives, as generally the case with the Slavs, being devoted to agriculture, the Germans became the traders. According to Lelewel, the Jews entered the country at the period of the Crusades.[1] They have ever since formed a very numerous element in the population. Thus the trade of Poland was entirely in the hands of foreigners, who were governed by a special code of laws, called the "Jus Magdeburgicum."

In the reign of Casimir the Great (1333—1370) Poland seems to have abandoned her hopes of

[1] Lelewel, i. 68.

amalgamating the western Slavs, and to have turned to the east.

In 1386 Lithuania was joined to Poland by the marriage of its prince, Jagiello, with the fair Hedwig, the Polish heiress, who consented to the union on political grounds as previously mentioned. The glory of Poland was at its height in the reign of Sigismund II. It was to decline thenceforward steadily, under the pernicious influence of the constant elections, scenes of fierce party strife and bloodshed, the *pacta conventa*, and, most of all, the *liberum veto*, viz., the power which one single nuntius had of stopping the proceedings of the diet. In the year 1488 the first printing-press was set up in Cracow, which was long far more the capital of the kingdom than Warsaw, and contains the tombs of its greatest monarchs. The feelings of the stranger are indeed melancholy when he contemplates these memorials of bygone grandeur. There, among others, lies Sigismund I., who nearly lost a crown through his love for the ill-starred Barbara Radzivill; and John Casimir, who, weary of the turmoils of state, abdicated that he might end his days as a French monk. There are to be found interred the timid Michael Korybut, who is said to have wept when the crown had been forced upon him by his fellow-nobles, and under a monument of black marble, bedecked with kneeling and chained Turks, that glory of Eastern Europe and *malleus Ottomanorum*—John Sobieski.

In Sigismund III. the Poles had a very ambitious king, who could aspire even to the crowns of Sweden and Russia. It is to him that Poland owes the great influence of the Jesuits. In his final speech to the diet, in 1668, when abdicating, John Casimir prophesied the evils which were gradually closing over the country ; and his predictions were fully verified. Before the glory of the country had set, there was the great splendour of the reign of Sobieski, who became the champion of the west against the east, and rescued Vienna from the Turks in 1683.[2] Sobieski died in 1686 ; his life had been a turbulent and an unhappy one ; he had neither peace in the meetings of the Diet, owing to the jealousy of the nobles, nor in the domestic circle, owing to the

[2] We see what a sensation this event created throughout Europe by such productions as the fine ode of Filicaia, addressed to him "Non perchè re sei tu, si grande sei."

brawls of his "charming Marie" with her children.

The whole period of the Saxon kings (1698—1763) was one of degradation, but material prosperity was not altogether wanting; and this is remembered in the well-known Polish proverb,—

> Za krola Sasa,
> Jedz, pij, popuszczaj pasa,
> A za krola Sobka
> Nie bylo w polu snopka,
>
> ---
>
> In the time of the Saxon king
> Eat, drink, loosen the girdle;
> But in the time of king Sobko (Sobieski)
> There was not a sheaf of wheat in the field.

While Poland was an independent kingdom, the Polish nationality had to struggle with many foreign elements—a fact which perhaps helps to explain its easy disintegration. Thus, the language of the greater part of Lithuania was not Polish; and there seems to have been always much jealousy between the two divisions of the country; the Cossacks and Ruthenians spoke a language of their own; and German, as previously mentioned, was prevalent in the large towns.

The Cossacks were, at an earlier period, divided into two great branches, those of the Don, and those of the Dnieper. The former were incorporated with Russia as early as the days of Ivan the Terrible; the latter, long nominally subjects to the Poles, broke out into rebellion under Bogdan Khmelnitzki about the middle of the seventeenth century, who, finding that he could not make head against the Polish generals, went over with all his followers to Alexis Mikhailovich, the father of Peter the Great. The western Cossacks established themselves on some islands of the Dnieper; their military republic has been already mentioned. Their numbers were recruited from renegade Poles, Little Russians, and Tatars, and their subjection to Poland was little more than nominal. The Poles invariably treated them with contempt, and severely punished their rebellions. A curious illustration of the opinion in which they were held, is furnished by Legnich in his " Jus Publicum Regni Poloni ;" after telling us that the soldiers had wished to have a vote in the election of the kings, but had been refused, he adds further, " Cosaci, qui in iisdem A. 1632 comitiis, idem quod milites expetebant, non sine indignatione audiebantur, *quod ex infimâ plebe colluvies nobilibus æquari vellent.* Hoc illis dato responso, quod neque ad electionem, neque ad ulla publica consilia pertinerent, sed esse Senatorum et nobilitatis de Republicâ agere."[3] The Cossacks were treated with severity by Peter the Great, especially after their hetman Mazepa had joined Charles XII. in his invasion of Russia. The hetmanship was abolished by Catherine II.

But in Poland all things were, as the ancients phrased it, præcipitia ad exitium. The country had no natural frontiers, and was surrounded on all sides by powerful enemies, the two most deadly of whom were the Russians, who were anxious to extend themselves towards the west, and the Prussians, who were covetous of the northern coast-line, and especially of the port of Danzig. A true middle class did not exist, the burgher element being, as previously mentioned, chiefly recruited from foreigners; there was nothing but a selfish and turbulent aristocracy of ecclesiastics and palatines, possessed of despotic power in their own territories; and at an infinite distance below them

[3] Vol. ii. p. 98.

a miserable body of serfs, who had no right of appeal against the tyranny of their masters. To the personal violence of the latter they were constantly exposed, and had, as we are assured in the accounts of those who visited the country during the time of its independence, a hopeless and downtrodden look. Meanwhile, in the palaces of their masters the wildest luxury reigned, and half-Asiatic barbarism was but thinly veneered by the French politeness which the fashionable Pole acquired in his travels.

This account of the miserable state of the Polish peasantry is fully corroborated by the interesting travels of Archdeacon Coxe. During the eighteenth century, the Polish serfs had sunk to the lowest depths of debasement. They knew nothing of State affairs or their governors, and it was a matter of indifference to them whether their masters obeyed the head of a Polish Republic, a Russian Empress, or a German King.[4] How great was the political corruption of the aristocracy we can see by such works as the " Fall of Poland,"

[4] Cf. Von Sybel, "French Revolution," English translation, vol. ii. p. 407.

by Soloviev, the Russian historian. The attempt made by a few patriots to stem the tide was useless, and in 1795, as all the world knows, Poland had ceased to exist as an independent country.

CHAPTER X.

POLISH LITERATURE.

THE Polish language has always been a great stumbling-block to Englishmen, and from its conglomerations of consonants and supposed harshness the very names of the leading authors who have written in Polish are unknown. Perhaps we must consider a native a prejudiced writer on such a subject; but if we wish for a vigorous defence of the language, let us listen to the eloquent words of Casimir Brodzinski, himself a poet of no mean order. "Let," he says, "the Pole smile with manly pride when the inhabitant of the banks of the Tiber or Seine calls his language rude; let him hear with keen satisfaction, and the dignity of a judge, the stranger who painfully struggles with the Polish pronunciation, like a Sybarite trying to lift an old Roman coat-of-armour, or when he struggles to articulate the language of men with the weak accent of children. While courage shall exist in our nation, while our manners shall not have become degraded, let us not disavow this manly roughness of our language. It has also its harmony, its melody; but it is the murmur of an oak of 300 years, and not the plaintive and feeble cry of a reed swayed by every wind!"

The following short notes on Polish literature will enable the reader to make himself acquainted with some of the chief names.

The earliest specimen (of any length) of the Polish language, is the so-called Psalter of Queen Margaret, discovered, in 1826, at the convent of St Florian, near Linz, in Austria, which dates from the middle of the fourteenth century. There is also an early hymn, or war-song (for it was a mixture of both), attributed to St. Adalbert of Prague, a great apostle among the Slavs. In 1347, the University of Cracow was founded—a city now incorporated with Austria. It still flourishes, and may be the ark for the preservation of the native language.

Many of the early Polish writers used Latin. The first poet who employed the tongue of the country was Rej, of Naglowic: most of his works are of a religious character, and would probably be more interesting to the antiquarian than the student of poetry. The influence of the renaissance was fully felt even in remote Poland. Jan Kochanowski, called the prince of Polish poets, was born in 1530. His culture was foreign, and chiefly acquired in Italy, and at the University of Padua. He gave his countrymen versions of Homer, Horace, and Cicero, and of the so-called Anacreontic Odes, which enjoyed such a popularity for many centuries. His "Treny," or Lamentations on the Death of a Favourite Daughter, who died in childhood, are much praised by Mickiewicz in his "Lectures on Slavonic Literature." The Kochanowskis were a poetical family: Andrew, the brother of John, translated the "Æneid" of Virgil; and his nephew Peter, the epics of Tasso and Ariosto.

In the sixteenth century we find mention of plays being first acted in Poland. To celebrate the marriage of Jan Zamoyski and Katherine Radziwill, on the 1st of January, 1578, a drama of Jan Kochanowski was represented; and in the year 1598, on the marriage of the bigoted Sigismund III. with

Anne of Austria, a comedy, called "The Labyrinth," was played.

During the eighteenth century a great deal of literature was produced in Poland, but none of a high character. About the middle of last century the most prominent Polish poet was Bishop Krasicki, the friend of Frederick the Great, and a prominent member of the King's Literary Club at Sans Souci. Krasicki attempted an epic, at a period of society probably the most unfavourable for epic composition ever known; for it was, we must remember, the age of the "Henriade," and Voltaire was the great poet of Europe. It must be confessed that the "War of Chozim," written to celebrate a Polish victory in the earlier part of the seventeenth century, is at best but a dull affair. The mock-heroics of Krasicki are, to say the least, amusing. Poems in the style of the "Rape of the Lock," are more likely to be genuine productions in the eighteenth century than an epic. Polish critics prefer to find the writings of the sportive bishop eminently national in tone; but into these niceties of criticism it is impossible for a foreigner to follow them. Besides his epic, we have his mock-heroic poem, entitled "Myszeis," where he describes how rats ate up the Polish king, Popiel—a legend found in all the early Polish chroniclers, and substantially the same as the story of Bishop Hatto, which forms the subject of one of Southey's most spirited ballads. His "Monachomachia" is in six cantos, and is, by some, considered his masterpiece. He is said to have written it at the suggestion of Frederick the Great, who told him that he had assigned him at Sans Souci the room which Voltaire had occupied, so that his poetical genius might be quickened.

So low had Polish literature sunk towards the end of the eighteenth century, that even translations of the feeble and insipid Delille—a kind of French Hayley—were in vogue among them. During this period Wegierski enjoyed a considerable reputation among his countrymen for his satirical writings. He appears to have been a kind of Polish Churchhill, and, like his English parallel, to have died young. In times of great national disaster, he deserves to be remembered as a genuine patriot. The poet laureate of the court of Stanislaus Augustus was Trembecki (1722—1812).

As the last period of Polish literature, the time

from the fall of the monarchy to our own day may be taken. Some of the most distinguished Polish writers have rendered this epoch of exile and proscription celebrated. Among these must be mentioned Julian Ursin Niemcewicz, born in Lithuania in 1758, died at Paris in 1841. Niemcewicz was not merely a poet. As a prototype of Körner and Petöfi, he fought bravely in the wars of his country as the adjutant of Kosciuszko, and went into captivity with him after Maciejowice, the Polish Chæronea. His most celebrated production is the "Collection of Historical Songs" (Spiewzy Historyczne), a series of lyrical compositions, in which the chief heroes of Polish history are introduced. The poet dwells with delight upon the golden age of Sigismund I., the reigns of Stephen Batory, and Sobieski. With the last of these, as with the fall of Polish greatness, the collection closes; one piece only being added, by way of supplement, entitled "The Funeral of Prince Joseph Poniatowski," one of Napoleon's marshals, drowned in the Elster after the battle of Leipzig.

The reputation, however, of Niemcewicz, considerable at the commencement of his own period, was destined to be far surpassed by that of Mickiewicz, confessedly one of the greatest of all Slavonic poets; Pushkin alone disputes the palm with him.

Adam Mickiewicz was born at Nowogrodek, near Wilno, in Lithuania, in 1798; his father, belonging to the szlachta, or lesser nobility, had an estate at this place. He was educated at the University of Wilno—since suppressed—and spent some time at St. Petersburg, where he made the acquaintance of many of the leading Russian literati. He afterwards obtained leave to travel, but had made up his mind never to return to Russia, and spent the rest of his life in exile, and chiefly at Paris. Of all the writings of Mickiewicz, his lyrical pieces are most beautiful, and show the language in its strength and grace. His works are but little known, except to his own countrymen; and there was both pathos and irony in the expression used by a Polish lady to a foreigner, "Nous avons notre Mickiewicz à nous." As yet no translation has appeared, as far as I am aware, of any production of the poet. There is a somewhat tame version in French prose by a compatriot, Christian Ostrowski, and Mickiewicz is said to have winced at the travesty of himself which had been accomplished by an honest admirer. His ballads are full of interest; their colouring is entirely national, treating of Lithuanian superstitions; as in " Switezianka," or wild adventures among the Cossacks of the Ukraine; as in " Czaty" (The Ambuscade).

The influence of the romantic school was now at its height throughout Europe; the torch had been kindled by Percy, in the " Reliques," and Scott, in the " Minstrelsy of the Scottish Border." The impression produced by these collections was first shown in Germany by the writings of Bürger and afterwards by Goethe and Schiller; and the *soil* of Poland was full of legend and picturesque histories, which only awaited the coming poet to put them into shape. But it took a long time to make these subjects fashionable; the battle of the classicists and romancists had to be fought out in Poland, as well as in other countries.

The sonnet was first introduced into Polish poetry by Mickiewicz, a fact alluded to with graceful words of compliment, by Pushkin, in one of his poems. The Crimean Sonnets are exquisitely finished compositions; the three most beautiful being "The Storm," "Bakche-Sarai," and "The Grave of the Countess Potocka." The last two pieces are written on the palace of the Khans of the Crimea, and the story of the Polish captive detained there, which forms the subject of Pushkin's fine poem, "The Fountain of Bakchi-Sarai." In "Konrad Wallenrod," a narrative poem detailing the battles of the Prussian Knights with the heathen Lithuanians, Mickiewicz disguised under a thin veil a representation of the sanguinary passages of arms, and burning hatred, which had characterized the long feuds of the Russians and Poles.

A slight sketch of the plot of this remarkable poem, which is very little known in this country may not be unwelcome to my readers. It opens with some spirited hexameters, narrating an expedition of the German knights to the banks of the Niemen. The time for the election of a new Grand Master has arrived, and the majority of the Order demand the nomination of Conrad Wallenrod, a mysterious man, who, although possessing great talent as a commander, is liable to occasional fits of melancholy. Konrad is elected, but all are disappointed in him; he spends his time indolently, and most of his expeditions result in disasters. Meanwhile, he has secret meetings with a lady living among the Lithuanians, who turns out to be his wife. After having ruined the cause of the Teutonic Knights, and when he is on the point of being put to death, he takes poison, and dies with the avowal that he is a Lithuanian, who has disguised himself, and has sought this means of avenging his country.

The story is unknown to many of the old writers (e.g., Hartknoch, "Alt- und Neues Preussen," 1684, who treats of Wallenrod among the other knights, and gives his portrait, but without any depreciatory remarks). Some of them, however, speak of him as a man to be abhorred; one says, "Er starb in Raserey, ohne letzte Oehlung, ohne Priestersegen." As a Lithuanian by birth, Mickiewicz naturally turned to the legends of his own country; and in the beautiful poem of "Grazyna" we have another piece on the wars between the knights and their heathen adversaries. This heroine, without the knowledge of her husband, goes disguised in armour, and rescues him when on the point of being slain by the German knights. She herself, however, is mortally wounded, and her body is brought to the castle. Preparations are made for burning the remains; and at the same time, according to the terrible custom prevailing among the Lithuanians, the captive chief of the Teutonic knights is brought to be consumed to ashes, still alive, on horseback, with all his arms, having been bound with three cords to a tree.[1] The prince discovers that the mysterious stranger is his own wife, and leaps into the flames. The poem of " Grazyna " is said by Ptrowski to have inspired the brave Emilia Plater, ho was the heroine of the revolution of 1830, and after having fought in the ranks of the insurgents, found a grave in the forests of Lithuania.

One of the longest and most celebrated pieces of Mickiewicz is his "Pan Tadeusz," by many considered to be his *chef-d'œuvre*, written in the year 1834. A curious picture is here given of Lithua-

[1] Mickiewicz, in his notes, quotes a curious passage from the Latin chronicler Stryikowski, who speaks of a victory gained by the Lithuanians and Samogitians over the knights in 1315, when Gerard Rudda, the starosta of the province of Sambia was burnt alive on horseback, clad in armour.

nia on the eve of Napoleon's great expedition to Russia in 1812. The poem is full of local colouring, and is worth hundreds of the productions of the Polish poets while under the influence of the so-called classical school and the rhetorical teaching of the Jesuits. To Mickiewicz it was a labour of love to describe the habits and scenes of his native country, Lithuania, which he was never to revisit. In 1855 he died suddenly, at Constantinople, whither he had been sent to assist in raising a Polish legion, to take service against the Russians during the Crimean war.

Since the death of the great poet, the romantic school, of which he may be said to have been almost the founder, has been further developed by the so-called Ukraine poets, especially Zaleski, Malczewski, Goszczynski, Padura, and Slowacki. The first is the writer of a poem of great elegance, "The Spirit of the Steppe" (Duch od Stepu). The inspiration is altogether from the Ukraine, one of the most picturesque parts of Russia, which has been praised in such enthusiastic terms by Gogol. The "Marya" of Malczewski is very much admired by the Poles, and has gone through many editions

It is a narrative poem, in the style of Byron. The opening is very spirited, but readers must not be expected to form an idea of a building from a solitary brick :—

Hey! Kossak on thy steed so fleet! say, whither art thou speeding?
Wilt thou hunt the hare thou seest, that o'er the steppe is bounding?
Wilt thou, in the play of thought, sport awhile with freedom?

The conclusion is pathetic, and the harmony of the Polish verses—for these Slavonic languages are wonderfully onomatopœic—is in strict accordance with the thought.

It is silent where the three graves show their sad and lonely hillocks!
It is gloomy now and desert amid the stormy Ukraine!

A poem of the same kind is the "Tower of Kaniow" (Zamek Kaniowski), by Goszczynski.

Padura has won fame as a poet, both in Polish and Ruthenish, or Red-Russian; his songs have especially earned him reputation among his countrymen. Slowacki, who died at Paris in 1849, was the author of a long poem, entitled "Beniowski," in the *ottava rima*, besides tragedies. Many of the productions of Constantine Gaszynski are of considerable merit, especially his sonnets, which he has modelled upon those of Mickiewicz. Another poet of considerable eminence is Lenartowicz, still living. His verses on the Nightingale are a proof of the extraordinary power of the Polish language in onomatopœia. Sigismund Krasinki, called "the unknown poet," was a writer of strange dreamy poems of considerable power, full of religious mysticism, such as "The Undivine Comedy" (Nieboska Komedja), "Irydion," and "Resurrecturis."

Polish prose has perhaps not been so successfully cultivated in modern times as poetry. It would, however, be unpardonable to omit the name of Lelewel, who occupies a very high place as a historian. Before the time of Lelewel, the most popular history of Poland was that by Waga, which is at best a mere compilation. Lelewel was originally a professor at Vilno, and while there Mickiewicz addressed a beautiful ode to him; but becoming involved in the political troubles of the year 1830, he was compelled to spend the rest of his days in exile, chiefly in Paris and Brussels. His

"History of Poland," of which there is a good translation in French, is divided into the following parts, the titles of which are significant:—Poland conquering, Poland divided, Poland flourishing, and Poland in its decadence.

A very valuable work is the "Monumenta Poloniæ Historica," edited at Lemburg, by Bielowski, of which two volumes have appeared. Here we have reprints of most of the early chroniclers. Bielowski died a year or so ago. The latest history of Poland is that by Röpell and Caro.

Altogether, in spite of so many years of political sufferings, the Poles still give signs of a vigorous nationality.

APPENDIX A.
RUSSIAN GOVERNMENTS.
EUROPE.

THE following list has been taken chiefly from Reclus, but only the most important towns are given, and I have not attempted to distinguish the various districts.

Baltic Provinces.

Esthonia—Revel, Hapsal.
Livonia—Riga, Dorpat.
Courland—Mittau.

Poland.

Warsaw—Warsaw (*Polish*, Warszawa).
Piotrkow—Piotrkow, Czestochowa.
Kalisz—Kalisz.
Kielce—Kielce.
Radom—Radom, Sandomierz.
Lublin.
Plock—Plock.
Lomza.
Suwalki.

Lithuania, Grodno, and Vitebsk.

Kovno—Kovno.
Vilno—Vilno, Troki.
Grodno—Grodno, Brest-Litovsk, Bielostok.
Vitebsk—Vitebsk, Polotzk, Dinaburg.

White, Little, and New Russia.

Smolensk—Smolensk, Dorogobouzh, Viazma.
Mogilov—Mogilov.
Minsk—Minsk, Borisov, Pinsk.
Volînia—Zhitomir, Lutzk, Ostrog.
Chernigov—Chernigov, Gloukhov.
Koursk—Koursk.
Kiev—Kiev, Berdíchev, Kanev.
Poltava—Poltava—Poltava, Kremenchoug, Perciaslavl.
Yekaterinoslav—Yekaterinoslav, Rostov, Taganrog.
Kherson—Kherson, Odessa.
Podolia—Kamenetz-Podolski.
Bessarabia—Kishenev.

Region of the Lakes.

Pskov—Pskov, Velikie Louki.
Novgorod—Novgorod, Tikhvin, Valdai.

St. Petersburg—St. Petersburg, Schlüsselbourg, Tzarskoe Selo, Kronstadt.

Olonetz—Petrzozavodsk, Korgopol.

Direction of the North.

Arkhangelsk—Arkhangelsk, Kholmogorî, Kola.

Vologda—Vologda, Veliki Oustiong.

Basin of the Volga.

Tver—Tver, Rzhev, Vishni-Volochok.

Kalouga—Kalouga, Borovsk, Maloyaroslavetz.

Moscow—Moscow, Kolomna, Serpoukhov.

Toula—Toula.

Orel—Orel, Briansk, Bolkhov.

Riazan—Riazan, Zaraisk, Kasimov.

Tambov—Tambov, Morshansk, Lipetzk.

Yaroslavl—Yaroslavl, Ouglich, Rostov.

Kostroma—Kostroma, Galich.

Vladímir—Vladímir, Souzdal.

Nizhni-Novgorod—Nizhni-Novgorod, Arzamas.

Penza—Penza, Mokshansk.

Kazan—Kazan, Christopol.

Viatka—Viatka, Slobodskoi.

Perm—Perm, Ekaterinenburg, Irbit.

Oufa—Oufa, Zlatoust.

Simbirsk—Simbirsk, Korsoun.
Samára—Samára, Sergievsk.
Sarátov—Sarátov, Tzaritzîn.
Astrakhan—Astrakhan, Tzarev.

Basin of the Oural.

Orenbourg—Orenbourg, Troitzk.

Basin of the Don.

Vorónezh—Vorónezh.
Kharkov—Kharkov.
Territory of the Army of the Don—Novo Cherkask.

Crimea and Continental Taurida.

Simferopol—Kerch, Sebastopol.

Grand Duchy of Finland.

Helsingfors, with the fortress Sveaborg, Abo.

ASIATIC RUSSIA.

Tobolsk—Tobolsk, Omsk, Berezov.
Tomsk—Tomsk, Bauaoul, Kornznetzk.
Yeniseisk—Krasnoyarsk, Yeniseisk, Kansk.
Irkutsk—Irkutsk, Troitzkosavsk, Kiakhta.

Yakutsk—Yakutsk, Okhotsk.
Zabaikalsk (Territory beyond Lake Baikal)—Chita, Nerchinsk.

Territory of Kamchatka.
Nizhnekamchatsk.

Tchukotsk. Territory of the Khirgiz.
Rumin.
Turkestan—Tashkend.

Territory of the Caucasus.
Tiflis—Tiflis, Yelisavetpol.
Kutais—Kutais, Akhaltzikh.
Erivan—Erivan, Nakhichevan, Alexandropol.
Shemakha—Shemakha, Batou.
Derbent—Derbent, Kouba.

Line of the Coast of the Black Sea.
By the treaty of Berlin, July 1878, which can be considered but little more than a temporary arrangement, Turkey cedes to Russia, Kars and the Port of Batoum, with the intervening and surrounding part of Armenia, to a line in about 40° N. latitude.

APPENDIX B.

The following works are recommended to those wishing to study the Geography, History, and Literature of Russia and Poland. I have made use of the greater part of them myself.

Reclus, E. : Nouvelle Géographie Universelle, vol. v., L'Europe—Scandinave et Russe. Paris, 1880. An admirable work, worthy of the great name of its author.

Solóviev : History of Russia (in Russian), 29 vols., reaching to the reign of the Empress Catherine.

Oustrialov : History of Russia. Two vols. 8vo. A very convenient work, full of well-condensed information, with excellent historical maps. In Russian. It has been of great service to me.

Ralston, W. R. : Early Russian History. London, 1874. An accurate and interesting little book.

Ralston, Russian Folk-Tales. London, 1873.

Ralston, The Songs of the Russian People, 1872.

Histoire de la Russie, par A. Rambaud. Paris, 1878.

Latham, R. G. : Native Races of the Russian Empire. 1854.

Rambaud : La Russie Épique. 1876.

Courrière, C. : Histoire de la Littérature Contemporaine en Russie.

Courrière, Histoire de la Littérature Contemporaine chez les Slaves. A useful book, but not always as accurate as could be desired.

Morfill, W. R. : Articles in the *Westminster Review*, October, 1877, and July, 1880, on Russian literature.

Wollner, Wilhelm : Untersuchungen über die Volksepik der Grossrussen. Leipzig, 1879.

Le Duc, Viollet : L'Art Russe. Paris.

Wallace, Mackenzie : Russia. London.

Svod Zakunov Slovanskych, Zporadal Dr. Hermenegild Jirecek : Collection of Slavonian Codes, edited by Dr. H. Jirecek. Prague, 1880.

Bestuzhev-Rioumin : History of Russia, of which there is a German translation.

Lelewel, J. : Histoire de Pologne. Two vols. Paris, 1844.

Cybulski, Dr. A. : Geschichte der Polnischen Dichtkunst. Posen, 1880.

Pypin and Spasovich : History of Slavonic Literature. In Russian, with German translation, by Traugott Pech.

INDEX.

AGRICULTURE, 141.
Alexander I., 165, 189.
Alexander II., 191.
Algarotti, 91.
Anglo-Saxon Chronicle, 52.
Animals, 28.
Anne, Empress, 186.
Architecture, 81.
Army, 139.
Art, 80.
Asiatic Russia, 20.
Asiatic Trade, 143.
Astrakhan, 113.

BAKOUNIN, 168, 169.
Bakchi-Sarai, 115.
Baltic, 3.
Baltic Finns, 33.
Batioushkov, 62.
Bells in Moscow, 97.
Beggars, 138.
Berezov, its climate, 23.
Black Sea Coast, 4.
Bogdanovich, 58.
Bomelius, Dr., 161.
Boris Godunov, 102, 182.
Bravery of Russian Soldiers, 156.
Brodzinski, 201.

Budini, 9.

CATHEDRALS, St. Isaac, 88; Kazan, 89; St. Michael, in Moscow, 95'; Assumption, 94.
Catherine II., 57, 188, 198.
Caucasus, 10.
Caucasian Races, 37.
Cereals, 27.
Chin, The, 124.
Churches in Moscow, 99.
Cis-Uralian Finns, 34.
Clarke, E. T., 97.
Clergy, 134, 136.
Coal, 147.
Codifications of Russian Laws, 123.
Condition of exiles in Siberia, 119.
Cossacks, 31, 140, 197.
Coxe, 199.

DERZHAVIN, 59.
Dignitaries, 124.
Dissenters, 134.
Dmitriev, 59.
Dnieper, 7.
Dniester, 6.
Domostroi, The, 177.
Don, 10.

Donalitius, 13.
Dress of peasants, 156.
Dvina, 14.
Dvina, Northern, 19.

ECCLESIASTICS, Number of, 137.
Elizabeth, Empress, 186.
Emperor, The, 121.
European Trade, 143.
Exports, 147.
Extent of Russia, 1.

FABULISTS, 66.
Fedkovich, 80.
Finland, 17; its privileges, 18, 123.
Finnish Dialects, 40.
Finnish Races, their divisions, 33.
Finns in the Governments of the Volga, 33.
Fruit, 28.

GERMANS in Russia, 38.
Gnedich's Homer, 63.
Gogol, 70.
Goszczynski, 212.
Great Russians, their distribution and numbers, 30.
Griboiedov, 59, 120.

HAKLUYT, 119.
Herberstein, 177.
Herzen, 166, 167.
Heylin, 176.
Horsey, Sir Jerome, 181.

ICONOGRAPHY, 82.
Ilya Murometz, 46.

Industries, 146.

Ivan the Terrible, 49, 95, 161, 175, 180, 182.

JAGIELLO, 194.
Jews, 38.
Jus Magdeburgicum, 193.

KALEVALA, the Finnish epic, 42.
Kalmuks, 35.
Karamzin, 60.
Khemnitzer, 58.
Kiev, 105, 108.
Kireev N., 155.
Kochanowski, John, Andrew, and Peter, 203.
Koltzov, 67.
Kotoshikin, 54.
Koubasov, 183.
Koulish, 75.
Kozlov, 107.
Krasicki, 204.
Krasinski, 214.
Kremlin, 92.
Krilov, 66.

LAKES, 5.
Le Duc, Viollet, 80.
Lelewel, 193.
Lenartowicz, 214.
Lermontov, 68.
Lettish language, 13.
Letts, their distribution and number, 33.
Literature, Russian, 44.
Lithuanians, 32.
Lithuanian language, 12.
Little Russians (Malorossiani), 30.
Lobnoe Miesto, 94.
Lomonosov, 54.

MALCZEWSKI, 212.
Malo-Russian Literature, 74, 79.
Manumission of the Serfs, 162.
Mickiewicz, 207, 209.
Mikoula Selianinovich, 46.
Minerals, 27.
Mongolian Invasion, 174.
Mongolo-Manzhourian Race, 34.
Monks, 133.
Moscow, 91—103; burnt by the Crim Tatars, 179.
Mountains, 5, 21.

NARVA, 15.
Natalia, 150.
Navy, 140.
Nekrasov, 71.
Nestor, 51, 106.
Neva, 15, 87.
Niemcewicz, 207.
Niemen, 11.
Nicholas, Emperor, 190.
Nihilism, 166.
Nizhni-Novgorod, 110.
Nobility, 125.
Non-Slavonic races, 32.
Novelists, 63.

OBI, 22.
Odessa, 108.
Onega River, 19.
Oural River, 11.
Oustriálov, 73.

PADURA, 212.
Painters, 84.
Paul, Emperor, 188.
Pechora River, 19.
Pestcherski, Monastery, 106.

Peter the Great, 184.
Peter II., 185.
Peter III., 187.
Petersburg, 86, 91.
Plater, Emilia, 211.
Polotzki, Simeon, 53.
Potemkin, 152.
Privy Council, 122.
Punishment of the Pravezh, 175.
Pushkin, 64, 66.

RALSTON, W.R.S., 159, 162.
Rje of Naglowic, 203.
Religions in Russia, 139.
Revel, 113.
Richelieu, Duc de, 109.
Riga, 111.
Röpell, 215.
Rousski Mir, 126, 133.
Runeberg, 17.
Rurik, 173.
Russia, Asiatic, 20.
Russian Dialects, 43.
Russian MS. in the Ashmolean Collection, 50.

SALTICHIKHA, The, 164.
Samarin, Youri, 155.
Samoyed, 34.
Schafarik, 61.
Schleicher, 42.
Schlusselburg, 16.
Schools, 84.
Scotch in Russia, 70.
Serfs, formerly treated with great cruelty, 164.
Sevastopol, 114.
Shevchenko, 77.
Siberia, 117.

Q

Slavonic family of languages, 42.
Slowacki, 213.
Sobieski, 195.
Social Life, 148.
Soloviev, 74.
Songs, 163.
Spread of the Russian Language, 2.
Superstitions, 159.
Suvorov, 89.
Sylvester, the Monk, 177.

TATARS, 90.
Tenure of Land, 126.
Tiflis, 120.
Tobolsk, 116.
Tolstoi, Count A., 65
Toula, 113.
Tourgheniev, 72.
Translations of English writers, 63.
Trans-Oural Finns, 34.
Trembecki, 203.
Troitza Monastery, 100.
Turko-Tatar Race, 36.

UNIVERSITIES, 85.

VENALITY of Russian Employés, 126.
Vilno, 104.
Vladimir, 172.
Volcanoes of Kamchatka, 20.
Volga, 10.
Von Visin, 58.

WALLENROD, 210.
Warsaw, 103, 104.
Weddings, 158.
Wegierski, 205.
White Russians, 8, 31.
White Russian Literature, 80.
Women, their position, 177.

YAIK River, 11.

ZALESKI, 212.
Zemstvo, The, 132.
Zhukovski, 61.

A Catalogue of American and Foreign Books Published or Imported by MESSRS. SAMPSON LOW & CO. *can be had on application.*

Crown Buildings, 188, Fleet Street, London,
January, 1881.

A Selection from the List of Books

PUBLISHED BY

SAMPSON LOW, MARSTON, SEARLE, & RIVINGTON.

ALPHABETICAL LIST.

A CLASSIFIED *Educational Catalogue of Works* published in Great Britain. Demy 8vo, cloth extra. Second Edition, revised and corrected to Christmas, 1879, 5s

About Some Fellows. By an ETON BOY, Author of "A Day of my Life." Cloth limp, square 16mo, 2s. 6d.

Adventures of Captain Mago. A Phœnician's Explorations 1000 years B.C. By LEON CAHUN. Numerous Illustrations. Crown 8vo, cloth extra, gilt edges, 7s. 6d.; plainer binding, 5s.

Adventures of a Young Naturalist. By LUCIEN BIART, with 117 beautiful Illustrations on Wood. Edited and adapted by PARKER GILLMORE. Post 8vo, cloth extra, gilt edges, New Edition, 7s. 6d.

Afghan Knife (The). A Novel. By ROBERT ARMITAGE STERNDALE, Author of "Seonee." Small post 8vo, cloth extra, 6s.

After Sundown; or, The Palette and the Pen. By W. W. FENN, Author of "Blind-Man's Holiday," &c. With Portrait of Author. 2 vols., crown 8vo, cloth extra, 24s.

Albania: A Narrative of Recent Travel. By E. F. KNIGHT. With some very good Illustrations specially made for the work. Crown 8vo, cloth extra, 12s. 6d.

Alcott (Louisa M.) Jimmy's Cruise in the " Pinafore." With 9 Illustrations. Second Edition. Small post 8vo, cloth gilt, 3s. 6d.

———— *Aunt Jo's Scrap-Bag.* Square 16mo, 2s. 6d. (Rose Library, 1s.)

———— *Little Men: Life at Plumfield with Jo's Boys.* Small post 8vo, cloth, gilt edges, 3s. 6d. (Rose Library, Double vol. 2s.)

———— *Little Women.* 1 vol., cloth, gilt edges, 3s. 6d. (Rose Library, 2 vols., 1s. each.)

A

Alcott (Louisa M.) Old-Fashioned Girl. Best Edition, small post 8vo, cloth extra, gilt edges, 3s. 6d. (Rose Library, 2s.)

—— *Work and Beginning Again.* A Story of Experience. 1 vol., small post 8vo, cloth extra, 6s. Several Illustrations. (Rose Library, 2 vols., 1s. each.)

—— *Shawl Straps.* Small post 8vo, cloth extra, gilt, 3s. 6d.

—— *Eight Cousins; or, the Aunt Hill.* Small post 8vo, with Illustrations, 3s. 6d.

—— *The Rose in Bloom.* Small post 8vo, cloth extra, 3s. 6d.

—— *Silver Pitchers.* Small post 8vo, cloth extra, 3s. 6d.

—— *Under the Lilacs.* Small post 8vo, cloth extra, 5s.

—— *Jack and Jill.* Small post 8vo, cloth extra, 5s.

"Miss Alcott's stories are thoroughly healthy, full of racy fun and humour . . . exceedingly entertaining . . . . We can recommend the 'Eight Cousins.'"—*Athenæum.*

Alpine Ascents and Adventures; or, Rock and Snow Sketches. By H. SCHÜTZ WILSON, of the Alpine Club. With Illustrations by WHYMPER and MARCUS STONE. Crown 8vo, 10s. 6d. 2nd Edition.

Andersen (Hans Christian) Fairy Tales. With Illustrations in Colours by E. V. B. Royal 4to, cloth, 25s.

Architecture (The Twenty Styles of). By Dr. W. WOOD, Author of "The Hundred Greatest Men." Imperial 8vo, with 52 Plates.

Art Education. See "Illustrated Text Books."

Autobiography of Sir G. Gilbert Scott, R.A., F.S.A., &c. Edited by his Son, G. GILBERT SCOTT. With an Introduction by the DEAN OF CHICHESTER, and a Funeral Sermon, preached in Westminster Abbey, by the DEAN OF WESTMINSTER. Also, Portrait on steel from the portrait of the Author by G. RICHMOND, R.A. 1 vol., demy 8vo, cloth extra, 18s.

THE BAYARD SERIES,

Edited by the late J. HAIN FRISWELL.

Comprising Pleasure Books of Literature produced in the Choicest Style as Companionable Volumes at Home and Abroad.

"We can hardly imagine better books for boys to read or for men to ponder over."—*Times.*

Price 2s. 6d. each Volume, complete in itself, flexible cloth extra, gilt edges, with silk Headbands and Registers.

The Story of the Chevalier Bayard. By M. De Berville.

De Joinville's St. Louis, King of France.

The Essays of Abraham Cowley, including all his Prose Works.

Abdallah; or, The Four Leaves. By Edouard Laboullaye.

The Bayard Series (continued):—

Table-Talk and Opinions of Napoleon Buonaparte.

Vathek: An Oriental Romance. By William Beckford.

The King and the Commons. A Selection of Cavalier and Puritan Songs. Edited by Professor Morley.

Words of Wellington: Maxims and Opinions of the Great Duke.

Dr. Johnson's Rasselas, Prince of Abyssinia. With Notes.

Hazlitt's Round Table. With Biographical Introduction.

The Religio Medici, Hydriotaphia, and the Letter to a Friend. By Sir Thomas Browne, Knt.

Ballad Poetry of the Affections. By Robert Buchanan.

Coleridge's Christabel, and other Imaginative Poems. With Preface by Algernon C. Swinburne.

Lord Chesterfield's Letters, Sentences, and Maxims. With Introduction by the Editor, and Essay on Chesterfield by M. de Ste.-Beuve, of the French Academy.

Essays in Mosaic. By Thos. Ballantyne.

My Uncle Toby; his Story and his Friends. Edited by P. Fitzgerald.

Reflections; or, Moral Sentences and Maxims of the Duke de la Rochefoucald.

Socrates: Memoirs for English Readers from Xenophon's Memorabilia. By Edw. Levien.

Prince Albert's Golden Precepts.

A Case containing 12 Volumes, price 31s. 6d.; or the Case separately, price 3s. 6d.

Beauty and the Beast. An Old Tale retold, with Pictures by E. V. B. 4to, cloth extra. 10 Illustrations in Colours. 12s. 6d.

Begum's Fortune (The): A New Story. By JULES VERNE. Translated by W. H. G. KINGSTON. Numerous Illustrations. Crown 8vo, cloth, gilt edges, 7s. 6d.; plainer binding, plain edges, 5s.

Ben Hur: A Tale of the Christ. By L. WALLACE. Crown 8vo, 6s.

Beumers' German Copybooks. In six gradations at 4d. each.

Biart (Lucien). See "Adventures of a Young Naturalist," "My Rambles in the New World," "The Two Friends," "Involuntary Voyage."

Bickersteth's Hymnal Companion to Book of Common Prayer may be had in various styles and bindings from 1d. to 21s. Price List and Prospectus will be forwarded on application.

Bickersteth (Rev. E. H., M.A.) The Reef, and other Parables. 1 vol., square 8vo, with numerous very beautiful Engravings, 2s. 6d.

—— *The Clergyman in his Home.* Small post 8vo, 1s.

—— *The Master's Home-Call; or, Brief Memorials of* Alice Frances Bickersteth. 20th Thousand. 32mo, cloth gilt, 1s.

—— *The Master's Will.* A Funeral Sermon preached on the Death of Mrs. S. Gurney Buxton. Sewn, 6d.; cloth gilt, 1s.

Bickersteth (Rev. E. H., M.A.) The Shadow of the Rock. A Selection of Religious Poetry. 18mo, cloth extra, 2s. 6d.

—— *The Shadowed Home and the Light Beyond.* 7th Edition, crown 8vo, cloth extra, 5s.

Biographies of the Great Artists (Illustrated). Each of the following Volumes is illustrated with from twelve to twenty full-page Engravings, printed in the best manner, and bound in ornamental cloth cover, 3s. 6d. Library Edition, bound in a superior style, and handsomely ornamented, with gilt top; six Volumes, enclosed in a cloth case, with lid, £1 11s. 6d. each case.

Hogarth.	Fra Bartolommeo.	Sir David Wilkie.
Turner.	Giotto.	Van Eyck.
Rubens.	Raphael.	Figure Painters of Holland.
Holbein.	Van Dyck and Hals.	
Tintoretto.	Titian.	Michel Angelo.
Little Masters of Germany.	Rembrandt.	Delaroche and Vernet.
	Leonardo da Vinci.	Landseer.
Fra Angelico and Masaccio.	Gainsborough and Constable.	Reynolds.

"Few things in the way of small books upon great subjects, avowedly cheap and necessarily brief, have been hitherto so well done as these biographies of the Great Masters in painting."—*Times.*

"A deserving series."—*Edinburgh Review.*

"Most thoroughly and tastefully edited."—*Spectator.*

Black (Wm.) Three Feathers. Small post 8vo, cloth extra, 6s.

—— *Lady Silverdale's Sweetheart, and other Stories.* 1 vol., small post 8vo, 6s.

—— *Kilmeny: a Novel.* Small post 8vo, cloth, 6s.

—— *In Silk Attire.* 3rd Edition, small post 8vo, 6s.

—— *A Daughter of Heth.* 11th Edition, small post 8vo, 6s.

—— *Sunrise.* 15 Monthly Parts, 1s. each.

Blackmore (R. D.) Lorna Doone. 10th Edition, cr. 8vo, 6s.

—— *Alice Lorraine.* 1 vol., small post 8vo, 6th Edition, 6s.

—— *Clara Vaughan.* Revised Edition, 6s.

—— *Cradock Nowell.* New Edition, 6s.

—— *Cripps the Carrier.* 3rd Edition, small post 8vo, 6s.

—— *Mary Anerley.* New Edition, 6s.

—— *Erema; or, My Father's Sin.* With 12 Illustrations, small post 8vo, 6s.

Blossoms from the King's Garden: Sermons for Children. By the Rev. C. BOSANQUET. 2nd Edition, small post 8vo, cloth extra, 6s.

Blue Banner (The); or, The Adventures of a Mussulman, a Christian, and a Pagan, in the time of the Crusades and Mongol Conquest. Translated from the French of LEON CAHUN. With Seventy-six Wood Engravings. Imperial 16mo, cloth, gilt edges, 7s. 6d.; plainer binding, 5s.

Boy's Froissart (The). 7s. 6d. *See* " Froissart."

Boy's King Arthur (The). With very fine Illustrations. Square crown 8vo, cloth extra, gilt edges, 7s. 6d. Edited by SIDNEY LANIER, Editor of " The Boy's Froissart."

Brazil: the Amazons, and the Coast. By HERBERT H. SMITH. With 115 Full-page and other Illustrations. Demy 8vo, 650 pp., 21s.

Brazil and the Brazilians. By J. C. FLETCHER and D. P. KIDDER. 9th Edition, Illustrated, 8vo, 21s.

Breton Folk: An Artistic Tour in Brittany. By HENRY BLACKBURN, Author of " Artists and Arabs," " Normandy Picturesque," &c. With 171 Illustrations by RANDOLPH CALDECOTT. Imperial 8vo, cloth extra, gilt edges, 21s.

Bricks without Straw. By the Author of " A Fool's Errand." Crown 8vo, with numerous Illustrations, 7s. 6d.

British Goblins: Welsh Folk-Lore, Fairy Mythology, Legends, and Traditions. By WIRT SYKES, United States Consul for Wales. With Illustrations by J. H. THOMAS. This account of the Fairy Mythology and Folk-Lore of his Principality is, by permission, dedicated to H.R.H. the Prince of Wales. Second Edition. 8vo, 18s.

Buckle (Henry Thomas) The Life and Writings of. By ALFRED HENRY HUTH. With Portrait. 2 vols., demy 8vo.

Burnaby (Capt.) See " On Horseback."

Burnham Beeches (Heath, F. G.). With numerous Illustrations and a Map. Crown 8vo, cloth, gilt edges, 3s. 6d. Second Edition.

Butler (W. F.) The Great Lone Land; an Account of the Red River Expedition, 1869-70. With Illustrations and Map. Fifth and Cheaper Edition, crown 8vo, cloth extra, 7s. 6d.

—— *The Wild North Land; the Story of a Winter Journey* with Dogs across Northern North America. Demy 8vo, cloth, with numerous Woodcuts and a Map, 4th Edition, 18s. Cr. 8vo, 7s. 6d.

—— *Akim-foo: the History of a Failure.* Demy 8vo, cloth, 2nd Edition, 16s. Also, in crown 8vo, 7s. 6d.

CADOGAN (Lady A.) Illustrated Games of Patience. Twenty-four Diagrams in Colours, with Descriptive Text. Foolscap 4to, cloth extra, gilt edges, 3rd Edition, 12s. 6d.

Caldecott (R.). See " Breton Folk."

Celebrated Travels and Travellers. See VERNE.

Changed Cross (The), and other Religious Poems. 16mo, 2s. 6d.

Child of the Cavern (The); or, Strange Doings Underground. By JULES VERNE. Translated by W. H. G. KINGSTON. Numerous Illustrations. Sq. cr. 8vo, gilt edges, 7s. 6d.; cl., plain edges, 5s.

Child's Play, with 16 Coloured Drawings by E. V. B. Printed on thick paper, with tints, 7s. 6d.
——— *New.* By E. V. B. Similar to the above. *See* New.
——— A New and Cheap Edition of the two above, containing 48 Illustrations by E. V. B., printed in tint, handsomely bound, 3s. 6d.
Children's Lives and How to Preserve Them ; or, The Nursery Handbook. By W. LOMAS, M.D. Crown 8vo, cloth, 5s.
Choice Editions of Choice Books. 2s. 6d. each, Illustrated by C. W. COPE, R.A., T. CRESWICK, R.A., E. DUNCAN, BIRKET FOSTER, J. C. HORSLEY, A.R.A., G. HICKS, R. REDGRAVE, R.A., C. STONEHOUSE, F. TAYLER, G. THOMAS, H. J. TOWNSHEND, E. H. WEHNERT, HARRISON WEIR, &c.

Bloomfield's Farmer's Boy.	Milton's L'Allegro.
Campbell's Pleasures of Hope.	Poetry of Nature. Harrison Weir.
Coleridge's Ancient Mariner.	Rogers' (Sam.) Pleasures of Memory.
Goldsmith's Deserted Village.	Shakespeare's Songs and Sonnets.
Goldsmith's Vicar of Wakefield.	Tennyson's May Queen.
Gray's Elegy in a Churchyard.	Elizabethan Poets.
Keat's Eve of St. Agnes.	Wordsworth's Pastoral Poems.

" Such works are a glorious beatification for a poet."—*Athenæum.*

Christ in Song. By Dr. PHILIP SCHAFF. A New Edition, Revised, cloth, gilt edges, 6s.
Cobbett (William). A Biography. By EDWARD SMITH. 2 vols., crown 8vo, 25s.
Confessions of a Frivolous Girl (The): A Novel of Fashionable Life. Edited by ROBERT GRANT. Crown 8vo, 6s.
Cradle-Land of Arts and Creeds ; or, Nothing New under the Sun. By CHARLES J. STONE, Barrister-at-law, and late Advocate, High Courts, Bombay. 8vo, pp. 420, cloth, 14s.
Cripps the Carrier. 3rd Edition, 6s. *See* BLACKMORE.
Cruise of H.M.S. " Challenger" (The). By W. J. J. SPRY, R.N. With Route Map and many Illustrations. 6th Edition, demy 8vo, cloth, 18s. Cheap Edition, crown 8vo, some of the Illustrations, 7s. 6d.
Curious Adventures of a Field Cricket. By Dr. ERNEST CANDÈZE. Translated by N. D'ANVERS. With numerous fine Illustrations. Crown 8vo, gilt, 7s. 6d.; plain binding and edges, 5s.

DANA (R. H.) Two Years before the Mast and Twenty-Four years After. Revised Edition, with Notes, 12mo, 6s.
Daughter (A) of Heth. By W. BLACK. Crown 8vo, 6s.
Day of My Life (A) ; or, Every Day Experiences at Eton. By an ETON BOY, Author of "About Some Fellows." 16mo, cloth extra, 2s. 6d. 6th Thousand.

Diane. By Mrs. MACQUOID. Crown 8vo, 6s.

Dick Cheveley: his Fortunes and Misfortunes. By W. H. G. KINGSTON. 350 pp., square 16mo, and 22 full-page Illustrations. Cloth, gilt edges, 7s. 6d.; plainer binding, plain edges, 5s.

Dick Sands, the Boy Captain. By JULES VERNE. With nearly 100 Illustrations, cloth, gilt, 10s. 6d.; plain binding and plain edges, 5s.

Dictionary (General) of Archæology and Antiquities. From the French of E. BOSC. Crown 8vo, with nearly 200 Illustrations, 10s. 6d.

Dodge (Mrs. M.) Hans Brinker; or, the Silver Skates. An entirely New Edition, with 59 Full-page and other Woodcuts. Square crown 8vo, cloth extra, 5s.; Text only, paper, 1s.

Dogs of Assize. A Legal Sketch-Book in Black and White. Containing 6 Drawings by WALTER J. ALLEN. Folio, in wrapper, 6s. 8d.

EIGHT Cousins. See ALCOTT.

Eighteenth Century Studies. Essays by F. HITCHMAN. Demy 8vo, 18s.

Elementary Education in Saxony. By J. L. BASHFORD, M.A., Trin. Coll., Camb. For Masters and Mistresses of Elementary Schools. Sewn, 1s.

Elinor Dryden. By Mrs. MACQUOID. Crown 8vo, 6s.

Embroidery (Handbook of). By L. HIGGIN. Edited by LADY MARIAN ALFORD, and published by authority of the Royal School of Art Needlework. With 16 page Illustrations, Designs for Borders, &c. Crown 8vo, 5s.

English Philosophers. Edited by IWAN MULLER, M.A., New College, Oxon. A Series of Volumes containing short biographies of the most celebrated English Philosophers, to each of whom is assigned a separate volume, giving as comprehensive and detailed a statement of his views and contributions to Philosophy as possible, explanatory rather than critical, opening with a brief biographical sketch, and concluding with a short general summary, and a bibliographical appendix. The Volumes will be issued at brief intervals, in square 16mo, 3s. 6d., containing about 200 pp. each.

The following are in the press:—

Bacon. Professor FOWLER, Professor of Logic in Oxford.
Berkeley. Professor T. H. GREEN, Professor of Moral Philosophy, Oxford.
Hamilton. Professor MONK, Professor of Moral Philosophy, Dublin.
[*Ready.*
J. S. Mill. HELEN TAYLOR, Editor of "The Works of Buckle," &c.

English Philosophers (continued) :—

Mansel. Rev. J. H. HUCKIN, D.D., Head Master of Repton.
Adam Smith. J. A. FARRER, M.A., Author of "Primitive Manners and Customs." [*Ready.*
Hobbes. A. H. GOSSET, B.A., Fellow of New College, Oxford.
Bentham. G. E. BUCKLE, M.A., Fellow of All Souls', Oxford.
Austin. HARRY JOHNSON, B.A., late Scholar of Queen's College, Oxford.
Hartley.⎱ E. S. BOWEN, B.A., late Scholar of New College,
James Mill.⎰ Oxford. [*Ready.*
Shaftesbury.⎱ Professor FOWLER.
Hutcheson.⎰

Arrangements are in progress for volumes on LOCKE, HUME, PALEY, REID, *&c.*

Episodes of French History. Edited, with Notes, Genealogical, Historical, and other Tables, by GUSTAVE MASSON, B.A.
    1. **Charlemagne and the Carlovingians.**
    2. **Louis XI. and the Crusades.**
    3. **Francis I. and Charles V.**
    4. **Francis I. and the Renaissance.**
The above Series is based upon M. Guizot's "History of France." Each volume is choicely Illustrated, with Maps, 2*s.* 6*d.*

Erema ; or, My Father's Sin. *See* BLACKMORE.

Etcher (The). Containing 36 Examples of the Original Etched-work of Celebrated Artists, amongst others: BIRKET FOSTER, J. E. HODGSON, R.A., COLIN HUNTER, J. P. HESELTINE, ROBERT W. MACBETH, R. S. CHATTOCK, H. R. ROBERTSON, &c., &c. Imperial 4to, cloth extra, gilt edges, 2*l.* 12*s.* 6*d.*

Eton. *See* "Day of my Life," "Out of School," "About Some Fellows."

Evans (C.) Over the Hills and Far Away. By C. EVANS. One Volume, crown 8vo, cloth extra, 10*s.* 6*d.*

——— *A Strange Friendship.* Crown 8vo, cloth, 5*s.*

Eve of Saint Agnes (The). By JOHN KEATS. Illustrated with Nineteen Etchings by CHARLES O. MURRAY. Folio, cloth extra, 21*s.* An Edition de Luxe on large paper, containing proof impressions, has been printed, and specially bound, 3*l.* 3*s.*

FARM Ballads. By WILL CARLETON. Boards, 1*s.* ; cloth, gilt edges, 1*s.* 6*d.*

Fern Paradise (The): A Plea for the Culture of Ferns. By F. G. HEATH. New Edition, entirely Rewritten, Illustrated with Eighteen full-page, numerous other Woodcuts, including 8 Plates of Ferns and Four Photographs, large post 8vo, cloth, gilt edges, 12*s.* 6*d.* Sixth Edition. In 12 Parts, sewn, 1*s.* each.

Fern World (The). By F. G. HEATH. Illustrated by Twelve Coloured Plates, giving complete Figures (Sixty-four in all) of every Species of British Fern, printed from Nature; by several full-page Engravings. Cloth, gilt, 6th Edition, 12s. 6d.

"Mr. HEATH has really given us good, well-written descriptions of our native Ferns, with indications of their habitats, the conditions under which they grow naturally, and under which they may be cultivated."—*Athenæum.*

Few (A) Hints on Proving Wills. Enlarged Edition, 1s.

First Steps in Conversational French Grammar. By F. JULIEN. Being an Introduction to "Petites Leçons de Conversation et de Grammaire," by the same Author. Fcap. 8vo, 128 pp., 1s.

Flooding of the Sahara (The). See MACKENZIE.

Food for the People; or, Lentils and other Vegetable Cookery. By E. E. ORLEBAR. Third Thousand. Small post 8vo, boards, 1s.

Fool's Errand (A). By ONE OF THE FOOLS. Author of Bricks without Straw. Crown 8vo, cloth extra, with numerous Illustrations, 8s. 6d.

Footsteps of the Master. See STOWE (Mrs. BEECHER).

Forbidden Land (A): Voyages to the Corea. By G. OPPERT. Numerous Illustrations and Maps. Demy 8vo, cloth extra, 21s.

Four Lectures on Electric Induction. Delivered at the Royal Institution, 1878-9. By J. E. H. GORDON, B.A. Cantab. With numerous Illustrations. Cloth limp, square 16mo, 3s.

Foreign Countries and the British Colonies. Edited by F. S. PULLING, M.A., Lecturer at Queen's College, Oxford, and formerly Professor at the Yorkshire College, Leeds. A Series of small Volumes descriptive of the principal Countries of the World by well-known Authors, each Country being treated of by a Writer who from Personal Knowledge is qualified to speak with authority on the Subject. The Volumes average 180 crown 8vo pages each, contain 2 Maps and Illustrations, crown 8vo, 3s. 6d.

The following is a List of the Volumes:—

Denmark and Iceland. By E. C. OTTE, Author of "Scandinavian History," &c.

Greece. By L. SERGEANT, B.A., Knight of the Hellenic Order of the Saviour, Author of "New Greece."

Switzerland. By W. A. P. COOLIDGE, M.A., Fellow of Magdalen College, Editor of *The Alpine Journal.*

Austria. By D. KAY, F.R.G.S.

Russia. By W. R. MORFILL, M.A., Oriel College, Oxford, Lecturer on the Ilchester Foundation, &c.

Persia. By Major-Gen. Sir F. J. GOLDSMID, K.C.S.I., Author of "Telegraph and Travel," &c.

Japan. By S. MOSSMAN, Author of "New Japan," &c.

Peru. By CLEMENTS H. MARKHAM, M.A., C.B.

Canada. By W. FRASER RAE, Author of "Westward by Rail," &c.

Foreign Countries (continued) :—

Sweden and Norway. By the Rev. F. H. WOODS, M.A., Fellow of St. John's College, Oxford.

The West Indies. By C. H. EDEN, F.R.G.S., Author of "Frozen Asia," &c.

New Zealand.

France. By Miss M. ROBERTS, Author of "The Atelier du Lys," "Mdlle. Mori," &c.

Egypt. By S. LANE POOLE, B.A., Author of "The Life of Edward Lane," &c.

Spain. By the Rev. WENTWORTH WEBSTER, M.A., Chaplain at St. Jean de Luz.

Turkey-in-Asia. By J. C. MCCOAN, M.P.

Australia. By J. F. VESEY FITZGERALD, late Premier of New South Wales.

Holland. By R. L. POOLE.

Franc (*Maude Jeane*). The following form one Series, small post 8vo, in uniform cloth bindings, with gilt edges:—

——— *Emily's Choice.* 5s.
——— *Hall's Vineyard.* 4s.
——— *John's Wife: a Story of Life in South Australia.* 4s.
——— *Marian; or, the Light of Some One's Home.* 5s.
——— *Silken Cords and Iron Fetters.* 4s.
——— *Vermont Vale.* 5s.
——— *Minnie's Mission.* 4s.
——— *Little Mercy.* 5s.
——— *Beatrice Melton's Discipline.* 4s.

Froissart (*The Boy's*). Selected from the Chronicles of England, France, Spain, &c. By SIDNEY LANIER. The Volume is fully Illustrated, and uniform with "The Boy's King Arthur." Crown 8vo, cloth, 7s. 6d.

GAMES of Patience. See CADOGAN.

Gentle Life (Queen Edition). 2 vols. in 1, small 4to, 10s. 6d.

THE GENTLE LIFE SERIES.

Price 6s. each; or in calf extra, price 10s. 6d.; Smaller Edition, cloth extra, 2s. 6d.

A Reprint (with the exception of "Familiar Words" and "Other People's Windows") has been issued in very neat limp cloth bindings at 2s. 6d. each.

The Gentle Life. Essays in aid of the Formation of Character of Gentlemen and Gentlewomen. 21st Edition.

"Deserves to be printed in letters of gold, and circulated in every house."—*Chambers' Journal.*

The Gentle Life Series (continued) :—

About in the World. Essays by Author of "The Gentle Life."
"It is not easy to open it at any page without finding some handy idea."—*Morning Post.*

Like unto Christ. A New Translation of Thomas à Kempis' "De Imitatione Christi." 2nd Edition.
"Could not be presented in a more exquisite form, for a more sightly volume was never seen."—*Illustrated London News.*

Familiar Words. An Index Verborum, or Quotation Handbook. Affording an immediate Reference to Phrases and Sentences that have become embedded in the English language. 4th and enlarged Edition. 6s.
"The most extensive dictionary of quotation we have met with."—*Notes and Queries.*

Essays by Montaigne. Edited and Annotated by the Author of "The Gentle Life." With Portrait. 2nd Edition.
"We should be glad if any words of ours could help to bespeak a large circulation for this handsome attractive book."—*Illustrated Times.*

The Countess of Pembroke's Arcadia. Written by Sir PHILIP SIDNEY. Edited with Notes by Author of "The Gentle Life." 7s. 6d.
"All the best things are retained intact in Mr. Friswell's edition."—*Examiner.*

The Gentle Life. 2nd Series, 8th Edition.
"There is not a single thought in the volume that does not contribute in some measure to the formation of a true gentleman."—*Daily News.*

The Silent Hour: Essays, Original and Selected. By the Author of "The Gentle Life." 3rd Edition.
"All who possess 'The Gentle Life' should own this volume."—*Standard.*

Half-Length Portraits. Short Studies of Notable Persons. By J. HAIN FRISWELL.

Essays on English Writers, for the Self-improvement of Students in English Literature.
"To all who have neglected to read and study their native literature we would certainly suggest the volume before us as a fitting introduction."—*Examiner.*

Other People's Windows. By J. HAIN FRISWELL. 3rd Edition.
"The chapters are so lively in themselves, so mingled with shrewd views of human nature, so full of illustrative anecdotes, that the reader cannot fail to be amused."—*Morning Post.*

A Man's Thoughts. By J. HAIN FRISWELL.

German Primer. Being an Introduction to First Steps in German. By M. T. PREU. 2s. 6d.

Getting On in the World; or, Hints on Success in Life. By W. MATHEWS, LL.D. Small post 8vo, cloth, 2s. 6d.; gilt edges, 3s. 6d.

Gilpin's Forest Scenery. Edited by F. G. HEATH. Large post 8vo, with numerous Illustrations. Uniform with "The Fern World," 12s. 6d. In 6 monthly parts, 2s. each.

Gordon (J. E. H.). See "Four Lectures on Electric Induction," "Physical Treatise on Electricity," &c.

Gouffé. The Royal Cookery Book. By JULES GOUFFÉ; translated and adapted for English use by ALPHONSE GOUFFÉ, Head Pastrycook to her Majesty the Queen. Illustrated with large plates printed in colours. 161 Woodcuts, 8vo, cloth extra, gilt edges, 2*l.* 2*s.*

―――― Domestic Edition, half-bound, 10*s.* 6*d.*

"By far the ablest and most complete work on cookery that has ever been submitted to the gastronomical world."—*Pall Mall Gazette.*

Great Artists. See "Biographies."

Great Historic Galleries of England (The). Edited by LORD RONALD GOWER, F.S.A., Trustee of the National Portrait Gallery. Illustrated by 24 large and carefully-executed *permanent* Photographs of some of the most celebrated Pictures by the Great Masters. Imperial 4to, cloth extra, gilt edges, 36*s.*

Great Musicians (The). A Series of Biographies of the Great Musicians. Edited by F HUEFFER.

1. **Wagner.** By the EDITOR.
2. **Weber.** By Sir JULIUS BENEDICT.
3. **Mendelssohn.** By JOSEPH BENNETT.
4. **Schubert.** By H. F. FROST.
5. **Rossini,** and the Modern Italian School. By H. SUTHERLAND EDWARDS.
6. **Marcello.** By ARRIGO BOITO.
7. **Purcell.** By H. W. CUMMINGS.

*** Dr. Hiller and other distinguished writers, both English and Foreign, have promised contributions. Each Volume is complete in itself. Small post 8vo, cloth extra, 3*s.*

Guizot's History of France. Translated by ROBERT BLACK. Super-royal 8vo, very numerous Full-page and other Illustrations. In 8 vols., cloth extra, gilt, each 24*s.*

"It supplies a want which has long been felt, and ought to be in the hands of all students of history."—*Times.*

―――――――― *Masson's School Edition.* The History of France from the Earliest Times to the Outbreak of the Revolution; abridged from the Translation by Robert Black, M.A., with Chronological Index, Historical and Genealogical Tables, &c. By Professor GUSTAVE MASSON, B.A., Assistant Master at Harrow School. With 24 full-page Portraits, and many other Illustrations. 1 vol., demy 8vo, 600 pp., cloth extra, 10*s.* 6*d.*

Guizot's History of England. In 3 vols. of about 500 pp. each, containing 60 to 70 Full-page and other Illustrations, cloth extra, gilt, 24*s.* each.

"For luxury of typography, plainness of print, and beauty of illustration, these volumes, of which but one has as yet appeared in English, will hold their own against any production of an age so luxurious as our own in everything, typography not excepted."—*Times.*

Guyon (Mde.) Life. By UPHAM. 6th Edition, crown 8vo, 6*s.*

*H*ANDBOOK to the Charities of London. *See* LOW'S.

—— of Embroidery ; which see.

—— to the Principal Schools of England. *See* Practical.

Half-Hours of Blind Man's Holiday ; or, Summer and Winter Sketches in Black and White. By W. W. FENN, Author of "After Sundown," &c. 2 vols., cr. 8vo, 24*s.*

Hall (W. W.) How to Live Long; or, 1408 *Health Maxims,* Physical, Mental, and Moral. By W. W. HALL, A.M., M.D. Small post 8vo, cloth, 2*s.* Second Edition.

Hans Brinker; or, the Silver Skates. See DODGE.

Harper's Monthly Magazine. Published Monthly. 160 pages, fully Illustrated. 1*s.* With two Serial Novels by celebrated Authors.

"'Harper's Magazine' is so thickly sown with excellent illustrations that to count them would be a work of time ; not that it is a picture magazine, for the engravings illustrate the text after the manner seen in some of our choicest *editions de luxe.*"— *St. James's Gazette.*

"It is so pretty, so big, and so cheap. . . . An extraordinary shillingsworth— 160 large octavo pages, with over a score of articles, and more than three times as many illustrations."—*Edinburgh Daily Review.*

"An amazing shillingsworth . . . combining choice literature of both nations."— *Nonconformist.*

Heart of Africa. Three Years' Travels and Adventures in the Unexplored Regions of Central Africa, from 1868 to 1871. By Dr. GEORG SCHWEINFURTH. Numerous Illustrations, and large Map. 2 vols., crown 8vo, cloth, 15*s.*

Heath (Francis George). See "Fern World," "Fern Paradise," "Our Woodland Trees," "Trees and Ferns," "Gilpin's Forest Scenery," "Burnham Beeches," "Sylvan Spring," &c.

Heber's (Bishop) Illustrated Edition of Hymns. With upwards of 100 beautiful Engravings. Small 4to, handsomely bound, 7*s.* 6*d.* Morocco, 18*s.* 6*d.* and 21*s.* An entirely New Edition.

Heir of Kilfinnan (The). New Story by W. H. G. KINGSTON, Author of "Snow Shoes and Canoes," &c. With Illustrations. Cloth, gilt edges, 7*s.* 6*d.* ; plainer binding, plain edges, 5*s.*

History and Handbook of Photography. Translated from the French of GASTON TISSANDIER. Edited by J. THOMSON. Imperial 16mo, over 300 pages, 70 Woodcuts, and Specimens of Prints by the best Permanent Processes. Second Edition, with an Appendix by the late Mr. HENRY FOX TALBOT. Cloth extra, 6*s.*

History of a Crime (The) ; Deposition of an Eye-witness. By VICTOR HUGO. 4 vols., crown 8vo, 42*s.* Cheap Edition, 1 vol., 6*s.*

—— *Ancient Art.* Translated from the German of JOHN WINCKELMANN, by JOHN LODGE, M.D. With very numerous Plates and Illustrations. 2 vols., 8vo, 36*s.*

—— *England. See* GUIZOT.

—— *France. See* GUIZOT.

History of Russia. See RAMBAUD.
——— *Merchant Shipping.* See LINDSAY.
——— *United States.* See BRYANT.
History and Principles of Weaving by Hand and by Power. With several hundred Illustrations. By ALFRED BARLOW. Royal 8vo, cloth extra, 1*l.* 5*s.* Second Edition.
How I Crossed Africa: from the Atlantic to the Indian Ocean, Through Unknown Countries; Discovery of the Great Zambesi Affluents, &c.—Vol. I., The King's Rifle. Vol. II., The Coillard Family. By Major SERPA PINTO. With 24 full-page and 118 half-page and smaller Illustrations, 13 small Maps, and 1 large one. 2 vols., demy 8vo, cloth extra, 42*s.*
How to Live Long. See HALL.
How to get Strong and how to Stay so. By WILLIAM BLAIKIE. A Manual of Rational, Physical, Gymnastic, and other Exercises. With Illustrations, small post 8vo, 5*s.*
Hugo (Victor) "*Ninety-Three.*" Illustrated. Crown 8vo, 6*s.*
——— *Toilers of the Sea.* Crown 8vo. Illustrated, 6*s.*; fancy boards, 2*s.*; cloth, 2*s.* 6*d.*; On large paper with all the original Illustrations, 10*s.* 6*d.*
———. See "History of a Crime."
Hundred Greatest Men (The). 8 portfolios, 21*s.* each, or 4 vols., half morocco, gilt edges, 12 guineas, containing 15 to 20 Portraits each. See below.
> "Messrs. SAMPSON LOW & Co. are about to issue an important 'International' work, entitled, 'THE HUNDRED GREATEST MEN;' being the Lives and Portraits of the 100 Greatest Men of History, divided into Eight Classes, each Class to form a Monthly Quarto Volume. The Introductions to the volumes are to be written by recognized authorities on the different subjects, the English contributors being DEAN STANLEY, Mr. MATTHEW ARNOLD, Mr. FROUDE, and Professor MAX MÜLLER: in Germany, Professor HELMHOLTZ; in France, MM. TAINE and RENAN; and in America, Mr. EMERSON. The Portraits are to be Reproductions from fine and rare Steel Engravings."—*Academy.*

Hygiene and Public Health (A Treatise on). Edited by A. H. BUCK, M.D. Illustrated by numerous Wood Engravings. In 2 royal 8vo vols., cloth, one guinea each.
Hymnal Companion to Book of Common Prayer. See BICKERSTETH.

ILLUSTRATED Text-Books of Art-Education. Edited by EDWARD J. POYNTER, R.A. Each Volume contains numerous Illustrations, and is strongly bound for the use of Students, price 5*s.* The Volumes now ready are:—

PAINTING.

Classic and Italian. By PERCY R. HEAD. With 50 Illustrations, 5*s.*

German, Flemish, and Dutch.
French and Spanish.
English and American.

Illustrated Text-Books (continued) :—

ARCHITECTURE.
Classic and Early Christian.
Gothic and Renaissance. By T. ROGER SMITH. With 50 Illustrations, 5s.

SCULPTURE.
Antique: Egyptian and Greek. | **Renaissance and Modern.**

ORNAMENT.
Decoration in Colour. | **Architectural Ornament.**

Illustrations of China and its People. By J. THOMPSON, F.R.G.S. Four Volumes, imperial 4to, each 3l. 3s.

In my Indian Garden. By PHIL ROBINSON, Author of "Under the Punkah." With a Preface by EDWIN ARNOLD, M.A., C.S.I., &c. Crown 8vo, limp cloth, 3s. 6d.

Involuntary Voyage (An). Showing how a Frenchman who abhorred the Sea was most unwillingly and by a series of accidents driven round the World. Numerous Illustrations. Square crown 8vo, cloth extra, 7s. 6d.; plainer binding, plain edges, 5s.

Irish Bar. Comprising Anecdotes, Bon-Mots, and Biographical Sketches of the Bench and Bar of Ireland. By J. RODERICK O'FLANAGAN, Barrister-at-Law. Crown 8vo, 12s. Second Edition.

Irish Land Question, and English Public Opinion (The). With a Supplement on Griffith's Valuation. By R. BARRY O'BRIEN, Author of "The Parliamentary History of the Irish Land Question." Fcap. 8vo, cloth, 2s.

Irving (Washington). Complete Library Edition of his Works in 27 Vols., Copyright, Unabridged, and with the Author's Latest Revisions, called the "Geoffrey Crayon" Edition, handsomely printed in large square 8vo, on superfine laid paper, and each volume, of about 500 pages, will be fully Illustrated. 12s. 6d. per vol. *See also* "Little Britain."

JACK and Jill. By Miss ALCOTT. Small post 8vo, cloth, gilt edges, 5s. With numerous Illustrations.

John Holdsworth, Chief Mate. By W. CLARKE RUSSELL, Author of "Wreck of the Grosvenor." Crown 8vo, 6s.

KINGSTON (W. H. G.). See "Snow-Shoes," "Child of the Cavern," "Two Supercargoes," "With Axe and Rifle," "Begum's Fortune," "Heir of Kilfinnan," "Dick Cheveley." Each vol., with very numerous Illustrations, square crown 16mo, gilt edges, 7s. 6d.; plainer binding, plain edges, 5s.

LADY Silverdale's Sweetheart. 6s. See BLACK.

Lenten Meditations. In Two Series, each complete in itself. By the Rev. CLAUDE BOSANQUET, Author of "Blossoms from the King's Garden." 16mo, cloth, First Series, 1s. 6d.; Second Series, 2s.

Library of Religious Poetry. A Collection of the Best Poems of all Ages and Tongues. With Biographical and Literary Notes. Edited by PHILIP SCHAFF, D.D., LL.D., and ARTHUR GILMAN, M.A. Royal 8vo, pp. 1036, cloth extra, gilt edges, 21s.

Life and Letters of the Honourable Charles Sumner (The). 2 vols., royal 8vo, cloth. Second Edition, 36s.

Lindsay (W. S.) History of Merchant Shipping and Ancient Commerce. Over 150 Illustrations, Maps, and Charts. In 4 vols., demy 8vo, cloth extra. Vols. 1 and 2, 21s.; vols. 3 and 4, 24s. each.

Little Britain; together with *The Spectre Bridegroom,* and *A Legend of Sleepy Hollow.* By WASHINGTON IRVING. An entirely New *Edition de luxe,* specially suitable for Presentation. Illustrated by 120 very fine Engravings on Wood, by Mr. J. D. COOPER. Designed by Mr. CHARLES O. MURRAY. Square crown 8vo, cloth extra, gilt edges, 10s. 6d.

Little King; or, the Taming of a Young Russian Count. By S. BLANDY. 64 Illustrations. Crown 8vo, gilt edges, 7s. 6d.; plainer binding, 5s.

Little Mercy; or, For Better for Worse. By MAUDE JEANNE FRANC, Author of "Marian," "Vermont Vale," &c., &c. Small post 8vo, cloth extra, 4s. Second Edition.

Lost Sir Massingberd. New Edition, crown 8vo, boards, coloured wrapper, 2s.

Low's German Series—
1. **The Illustrated German Primer.** Being the easiest introduction to the study of German for all beginners. 1s.
2. **The Children's own German Book.** A Selection of Amusing and Instructive Stories in Prose. Edited by Dr. A. L. MEISSNER. Small post 8vo, cloth, 1s. 6d.
3. **The First German Reader, for Children from Ten to Fourteen.** Edited by Dr. A. L. MEISSNER. Small post 8vo, cloth, 1s. 6d.
4. **The Second German Reader.** Edited by Dr. A. L. MEISSNER. Small post 8vo, cloth, 1s. 6d.

    Buchheim's Deutsche Prosa. Two Volumes, sold separately:—
5. **Schiller's Prosa.** Containing Selections from the Prose Works of Schiller, with Notes for English Students. By Dr. BUCHHEIM. Small post 8vo, 2s. 6d.
6. **Goethe's Prosa.** Selections from the Prose Works of Goethe, with Notes for English Students. By Dr. BUCHHEIM. Small post 8vo, 3s. 6d.

Low's International Series of Toy Books. 6*d.* each; or Mounted on Linen, 1*s.*

1. **Little Fred and his Fiddle,** from Asbjörnsen's "Norwegian Fairy Tales."
2. **The Lad and the North Wind,** ditto.
3. **The Pancake,** ditto.
4. **The Little Match Girl,** from H. C. Andersen's "Danish Fairy Tales."
5. **The Emperor's New Clothes,** ditto.
6. **The Gallant Tin Soldier,** ditto.

The above in 1 vol., cloth extra, gilt edges, with the whole 36 Coloured Illustrations, 5*s.*

Low's Standard Library of Travel and Adventure. Crown 8vo, bound uniformly in cloth extra, price 7*s.* 6*d.*

1. **The Great Lone Land.** By Major W. F. BUTLER, C.B.
2. **The Wild North Land.** By Major W. F. BUTLER, C.B.
3. **How I found Livingstone.** By H. M. STANLEY.
4. **The Threshold of the Unknown Region.** By C. R. MARKHAM. (4th Edition, with Additional Chapters, 10*s.* 6*d.*)
5. **A Whaling Cruise to Baffin's Bay and the Gulf of Boothia.** By A. H. MARKHAM.
6. **Campaigning on the Oxus.** By J. A. MACGAHAN.
7. **Akim-foo: the History of a Failure.** By MAJOR W. F. BUTLER, C.B.
8. **Ocean to Ocean.** By the Rev. GEORGE M. GRANT. With Illustrations.
9. **Cruise of the Challenger.** By W. J. J. SPRY, R.N.
10. **Schweinfurth's Heart of Africa.** 2 vols., 15*s.*
11. **Through the Dark Continent.** By H. M. STANLEY. 1 vol., 12*s.* 6*d.*

Low's Standard Novels. Crown 8vo, 6*s.* each, cloth extra.

My Lady Greensleeves. By HELEN MATHERS, Authoress of "Comin' through the Rye," "Cherry Ripe," &c.
Three Feathers. By WILLIAM BLACK.
A Daughter of Heth. 13th Edition. By W. BLACK. With Frontispiece by F. WALKER, A.R.A.
Kilmeny. A Novel. By W. BLACK.
In Silk Attire. By W. BLACK.
Lady Silverdale's Sweetheart. By W. BLACK.
History of a Crime: The Story of the Coup d'Etat. By VICTOR HUGO.

Low's Standard Novels (continued) :—

Alice Lorraine. By R. D. BLACKMORE.
Lorna Doone. By R. D. BLACKMORE. 8th Edition.
Cradock Nowell. By R. D. BLACKMORE.
Clara Vaughan. By R. D. BLACKMORE.
Cripps the Carrier. By R. D. BLACKMORE.
Erema; or, My Father's Sin. By R. D. BLACKMORE.
Mary Anerley. By R. D. BLACKMORE.
Innocent. By Mrs. OLIPHANT. Eight Illustrations.
Work. A Story of Experience. By LOUISA M. ALCOTT. Illustrations. *See also* Rose Library.
The Afghan Knife. By R. A. STERNDALE, Author of "Seonee."
A French Heiress in her own Chateau. By the Author of "One Only," "Constantia," &c. Six Illustrations.
Ninety-Three. By VICTOR HUGO. Numerous Illustrations.
My Wife and I. By Mrs. BEECHER STOWE.
Wreck of the Grosvenor. By W. CLARK RUSSELL.
John Holdsworth (Chief Mate). By W. CLARK RUSSELL.
Elinor Dryden. By Mrs. MACQUOID.
Diane. By Mrs. MACQUOID.
Poganuc People, Their Loves and Lives. By Mrs. BEECHER STOWE.
A Golden Sorrow. By Mrs. CASHEL HOEY.
A Story of the Dragonnades; or, Asylum Christi. By the Rev. E. GILLIAT, M.A.

Low's Handbook to the Charities of London. Edited and revised to date by C. MACKESON, F.S.S., Editor of "A Guide to the Churches of London and its Suburbs," &c. Paper, 1s.; cloth, 1s. 6d.

MACGAHAN (J. A.) Campaigning on the Oxus, and the Fall of Khiva. With Map and numerous Illustrations, 4th Edition, small post 8vo, cloth extra, 7s. 6d.

Macgregor (John) "Rob Roy" on the Baltic. 3rd Edition, small post 8vo, 2s. 6d.; cloth, gilt edges, 3s. 6d.

―――― *A Thousand Miles in the "Rob Roy" Canoe.* 11th Edition, small post 8vo, 2s. 6d.; cloth, gilt edges, 3s. 6d.

―――― *Description of the "Rob Roy" Canoe*, with Plans, &c., 1s.

―――― *The Voyage Alone in the Yawl "Rob Roy."* New Edition, thoroughly revised, with additions, small post 8vo, 5s.; boards, 2s. 6d.

Mackenzie (D.) The Flooding of the Sahara. By DONALD MACKENZIE. 8vo, cloth extra, with Illustrations, 10s. 6d.

Macquoid (Mrs.) Elinor Dryden. Crown 8vo, cloth, 6s.

—— *Diane.* Crown 8vo, 6s.

Magazine. *See* HARPER.

Markham (C. R.) The Threshold of the Unknown Region. Crown 8vo, with Four Maps, 4th Edition. Cloth extra, 10s. 6d.

Maury (Commander) Physical Geography of the Sea, and its Meteorology. Being a Reconstruction and Enlargement of his former Work, with Charts and Diagrams. New Edition, crown 8vo, 6s.

Memoirs of Count Miot de Melito. 2 vols., demy 8vo, 36s.

Memoirs of Madame de Rémusat, 1802—1808. By her Grandson, M. PAUL DE RÉMUSAT, Senator. Translated by Mrs. CASHEL HOEY and Mr. JOHN LILLIE. 4th Edition, cloth extra. This work was written by Madame de Rémusat during the time she was living on the most intimate terms with the Empress Josephine, and is full of revelations respecting the private life of Bonaparte, and of men and politics of the first years of the century. Revelations which have already created a great sensation in Paris. 8vo, 2 vols., 32s.

Menus (366, one for each day of the year). Translated from the French of COUNT BRISSE, by Mrs. MATTHEW CLARKE. Crown 8vo, 10s. 6d.

Men of Mark: a Gallery of Contemporary Portraits of the most Eminent Men of the Day taken from Life, especially for this publication, price 1s. 6d. monthly. Vols. I., II., III., IV., and V., handsomely bound, cloth, gilt edges, 25s. each.

Mendelssohn Family (The). Translated from the German of E. BOCK. Demy 8vo, 16s.

Michael Strogoff. 10s. 6d. and 5s. *See* VERNE.

Mitford (Miss). *See* "Our Village."

Military Maxims. By CAPTAIN B. TERLING. Medium 16mo, in roan case, with pencil for the pocket, 10s. 6d.

Mountain and Prairie: a Journey from Victoria to Winnipeg, viâ Peace River Pass. By the Rev. DANIEL M. GORDON, B.D., Ottawa. Small post 8vo, with Maps and Illustrations, cloth extra, 8s. 6d.

Music. *See* "Great Musicians."

My Lady Greensleeves. By HELEN MATHERS, Authoress of "Comin' through the Rye," "Cherry Ripe," &c. 1 vol. edition, crown 8vo, cloth, 6s.

Mysterious Island. By JULES VERNE. 3 vols., imperial 16mo. 150 Illustrations, cloth gilt, 3s. 6d. each; elaborately bound, gilt edges, 7s. 6d. each. Cheap Edition, with some of the Illustrations, cloth, gilt, 2s.; paper, 1s. each.

NATIONAL Music of the World. By the late HENRY F. CHORLEY. Edited by H. G. HEWLETT. Crown 8vo, cloth, 8s. 6d.

Naval Brigade in South Africa (The). By HENRY F. NORBURY, C.B., R.N. Crown 8vo, cloth extra, 10s. 6d.

New Child's Play (A). Sixteen Drawings by E. V. B. Beautifully printed in colours, 4to, cloth extra, 12s. 6d.

New Guinea (A Few Months in). By OCTAVIUS C. STONE, F.R.G.S. With numerous Illustrations from the Author's own Drawings. Crown 8vo, cloth, 12s.

—————— *What I did and what I saw.* By L. M. D'ALBERTIS, Officer of the Order of the Crown of Italy, Honorary Member and Gold Medallist of the I.R.G S., C.M.Z.S., &c., &c. In 2 vols., demy 8vo, cloth extra, with Maps, Coloured Plates, and numerous very fine Woodcut Illustrations, 42s.

New Ireland. By A. M. SULLIVAN, M.P. for Louth. 2 vols., demy 8vo, 30s. Cheaper Edition, 1 vol., crown 8vo, 8s. 6d.

New Novels. Crown 8vo, cloth, 10s. 6d. per vol. :—

Mary Marston. By GEORGE MACDONALD. 3 vols. Third Edition
Sarah de Beranger. By JEAN INGELOW. 3 vols.
Don John. By JEAN INGELOW. 3 vols.
Sunrise: A Story of these Times. By WILLIAM BLACK. 3 vols.
A Sailor's Sweetheart. By W. CLARK RUSSELL, Author of "The Wreck of the Grosvenor," "John Holdsworth," &c. 3 vols.
Lisa Lena. By EDWARD JENKINS, Author of "Ginx's Baby." 2 vols.
A Plot of the Present Day. By KATE HOPE. 3 vols.
Black Abbey. By M. CROMMELIN, Author of "Queenie," &c. 3 vols.
Flower o' the Broom. By the Author of "Rare Pale Margaret," 3 vols.
The Grandidiers: A Tale of Berlin. Translated from the German by Captain WM. SAVILE. 3 vols.
Errant: A Life Story of Latter-Day Chivalry. By PERCY GREG, Author of "Across the Zodiac," &c. 3 vols.
Fancy Free. By C. GIBBON. 3 vols.
The Stillwater Tragedy. By J. B. ALDRICH.
Prince Fortune and Prince Fatal. By Mrs. CARRINGTON, Author of "My Cousin Maurice," &c. 3 vols.

New Novels (continued) :—
> **An English Squire.** By C. B. COLERIDGE, Author of "Lady Betty," "Hanbury Wills," &c. 3 vols.
> **Christowell.** By R. D. BLACKMORE. 3 vols.
> **Mr. Caroli.** By Miss SEGUIN. 3 vols.
> **David Broome, Artist.** By Miss O'REILLY. 3 vols.
> **Braes of Yarrow.** By CHAS. GIBBON. 3 vols.

Nice and Her Neighbours. By the Rev. CANON HOLE, Author of "A Book about Roses," "A Little Tour in Ireland," &c. Small 4to, with numerous choice Illustrations, 12s. 6d.

Noble Words and Noble Deeds. From the French of E. MULLER. Containing many Full-page Illustrations by PHILIPPOTEAUX. Square imperial 16mo, cloth extra, 7s. 6d.; plainer binding, plain edges, 5s.

North American Review (The). Monthly, price 2s. 6d.

Nothing to Wear; and Two Millions. By W. A. BUTLER. New Edition. Small post 8vo, in stiff coloured wrapper, 1s.

Nursery Playmates (Prince of). 217 Coloured pictures for Children by eminent Artists. Folio, in coloured boards, 6s.

OBERAMMERGAU Passion Play. See "Art in the Mountains."

O'Brien. See "Parliamentary History" and "Irish Land Question."

Old-Fashioned Girl. See ALCOTT.

On Horseback through Asia Minor. By Capt. FRED BURNABY, Royal Horse Guards, Author of "A Ride to Khiva." 2 vols., 8vo, with three Maps and Portrait of Author, 6th Edition, 38s.; Cheaper Edition, crown 8vo, 10s. 6d.

Our Little Ones in Heaven. Edited by the Rev. H. ROBBINS. With Frontispiece after Sir JOSHUA REYNOLDS. Fcap., cloth extra, New Edition—the 3rd, with Illustrations, 5s.

Our Village. By MARY RUSSELL MITFORD. Illustrated with Frontispiece Steel Engraving, and 12 full-page and 157 smaller Cuts of Figure Subjects and Scenes. Crown 4to, cloth, gilt edges, 21s.

Our Woodland Trees. By F. G. HEATH. Large post 8vo, cloth, gilt edges, uniform with "Fern World" and "Fern Paradise," by the same Author. 8 Coloured Plates (showing leaves of every British Tree) and 20 Woodcuts, cloth, gilt edges, 12s. 6d. Third Edition.

Painters of All Schools. By LOUIS VIARDOT, and other Writers. 500 pp., super-royal 8vo, 20 Full-page and 70 smaller Engravings, cloth extra, 25s. A New Edition is issued in Half-crown parts, with fifty additional portraits, cloth, gilt edges, 31s. 6d.

Painting (A Short History of the British School of). By GEO. H. SHEPHERD. Post 8vo, cloth, 3s. 6d.

Palliser (Mrs.) A History of Lace, from the Earliest Period. A New and Revised Edition, with additional cuts and text, upwards of 100 Illustrations and coloured Designs. 1 vol., 8vo, 1l. 1s.

—— *Historic Devices, Badges, and War Cries.* 8vo, 1l. 1s.

—— *The China Collector's Pocket Companion.* With upwards of 1000 Illustrations of Marks and Monograms. 2nd Edition, with Additions. Small post 8vo, limp cloth, 5s.

Parliamentary History of the Irish Land Question (The). From 1829 to 1869, and the Origin and Results of the Ulster Custom. By R. BARRY O'BRIEN, Barrister-at-Law, Author of "The Irish Land Question and English Public Opinion." 3rd Edition, corrected and revised, with additional matter. Post 8vo, cloth extra, 6s.

The Right Hon. W. E. GLADSTONE, M.P., in a Letter to the Author, says:— "I thank you for kindly sending me your work, and I hope that the sad and discreditable story which you have told so well in your narrative of the Irish Land Question may be useful at a period when we have more than ever of reason to desire that it should be thoroughly understood."

Pathways of Palestine: a Descriptive Tour through the Holy Land. By the Rev. CANON TRISTRAM. Illustrated with 44 permanent Photographs. (The Photographs are large, and most perfect Specimens of the Art.) Published in 22 Monthly Parts, 4to, in Wrapper, 2s. 6d. each.

"... The Photographs which illustrate these pages may justly claim, as works of art, to be the most admirably executed views which have been produced. ...

"As the writer is on the point of making a fourth visit of exploration to the country, any new discoveries which come under observation will be at once incorporated in this work."

Peasant Life in the West of England. By FRANCIS GEORGE HEATH, Author of "Sylvan Spring," "The Fern World." Crown 8vo, about 350 pp., 10s. 6d.

Petites Leçons de Conversation et de Grammaire: Oral and Conversational Method; being Lessons introducing the most Useful Topics of Conversation, upon an entirely new principle, &c. By F. JULIEN, French Master at King Edward the Sixth's School, Birmingham. Author of "The Student's French Examiner," "First Steps in Conversational French Grammar," which see.

Phillips (L.) Dictionary of Biographical Reference. 8vo, 1l. 11s. 6d.

Photography (History and Handbook of). See TISSANDIER.

Physical Treatise on Electricity and Magnetism. By J. E. H. GORDON, B.A. With about 200 coloured, full-page, and other Illustrations. Among the newer portions of the work may be enumerated: All the more recent investigations on Striæ by Spottiswoode, De la Rue, Moulton, &c., an account of Mr. Crooke's recent researches; full descriptions and pictures of all the modern Magnetic Survey Instruments now used at Kew Observatory; full accounts of all the modern work on Specific Inductive Capacity, and of the more recent determination of the ratio of Electric units (v). In respect to the number and beauty of the Illustrations, the work is quite unique. 2 vols., 8vo, 36s.

Pinto (Major Serpa). See "How I Crossed Africa."

Plutarch's Lives. An Entirely New and Library Edition. Edited by A. H. CLOUGH, Esq. 5 vols., 8vo, 2l. 10s.; half-morocco, gilt top, 3l. Also in 1 vol., royal 8vo, 800 pp., cloth extra, 18s.; half-bound, 21s.

Poems of the Inner Life. A New Edition, Revised, with many additional Poems. Small post 8vo, cloth, 5s.

Poganuc People: their Loves and Lives. By Mrs. BEECHER STOWE. Crown 8vo, cloth, 6s.

Polar Expeditions. See KOLDEWEY, MARKHAM, MACGAHAN, and NARES.

Poynter (Edward J., R.A.). See "Illustrated Text-books."

Practical (A) Handbook to the Principal Schools of England. By C. E. PASCOE. New Edition, crown 8vo, cloth extra, 3s. 6d.

Prejevalsky (N. M.) From Kulja, across the Tian Shan to Lobnor. Translated by E. DELMAR MORGAN, F.R.G.S. Demy 8vo, with a Map. 16s.

Primitive Folk Moots; or, Open-Air Assemblies in Britain. By GEORGE LAURENCE GOMME, F.S.A., Honorary Secretary to the Folk-Lore Society, Author of "Index of Municipal Offices." 1 vol., crown 8vo, cloth, 12s.

This work deals with an earlier phase of the history of English Institutions than has yet been attempted.

Publishers' Circular (The), and General Record of British and Foreign Literature. Published on the 1st and 15th of every Month, 3d.

Pyrenees (The). By HENRY BLACKBURN. With 100 Illustrations by GUSTAVE DORÉ, a New Map of Routes, and Information for Travellers, corrected to 1881. With a description of Lourdes in 1880. Crown 8vo, cloth extra, 7s. 6d.

Rambaud (Alfred). History of Russia, from its Origin to the Year 1877. With Six Maps. Translated by Mrs. L. B. Lang. 2 vols., demy 8vo, cloth extra, 38s.

Recollections of Writers. By CHARLES and MARY COWDEN CLARKE. Authors of "The Concordance to Shakespeare," &c.; with Letters of CHARLES LAMB, LEIGH HUNT, DOUGLAS JERROLD, and CHARLES DICKENS; and a Preface by MARY COWDEN CLARKE. Crown 8vo, cloth, 10s. 6d.

Rémusat (Madame de). See "Memoirs of."

Robinson (Phil). See "In my Indian Garden," "Under the Punkah."

Rochefoucauld's Reflections. Bayard Series, 2s. 6d.

Rogers (S.) Pleasures of Memory. See "Choice Editions of Choice Books." 2s. 6d.

Rose in Bloom. See ALCOTT.

The Rose Library. Popular Literature of all countries. Each volume, 1s.; cloth, 2s. 6d. Many of the Volumes are Illustrated—

1. **Sea-Gull Rock.** By JULES SANDEAU. Illustrated.
2. **Little Women.** By LOUISA M. ALCOTT.
3. **Little Women Wedded.** Forming a Sequel to "Little Women."
4. **The House on Wheels.** By MADAME DE STOLZ. Illustrated.
5. **Little Men.** By LOUISA M. ALCOTT. Dble. vol., 2s.; cloth, 3s. 6d.
6. **The Old-Fashioned Girl.** By LOUISA M. ALCOTT. Double vol., 2s.; cloth, 3s. 6d.
7. **The Mistress of the Manse.** By J. G. HOLLAND.
8. **Timothy Titcomb's Letters to Young People, Single and Married.**
9. **Undine, and the Two Captains.** By Baron DE LA MOTTE FOUQUÉ. A New Translation by F. E. BUNNETT. Illustrated.
10. **Draxy Miller's Dowry, and the Elder's Wife.** By SAXE HOLM.
11. **The Four Gold Pieces.** By Madame GOURAUD. Numerous Illustrations.
12. **Work.** A Story of Experience. First Portion. By LOUISA M. ALCOTT.
13. **Beginning Again.** Being a Continuation of "Work." By LOUISA M. ALCOTT.
14. **Picciola; or, the Prison Flower.** By X. B. SAINTINE. Numerous Graphic Illustrations.

The Rose Library (continued) :—

15. **Robert's Holidays.** Illustrated.
16. **The Two Children of St. Domingo.** Numerous Illustrations.
17. **Aunt Jo's Scrap Bag.**
18. **Stowe (Mrs. H. B.) The Pearl of Orr's Island.**
19. ——— **The Minister's Wooing.**
20. ——— **Betty's Bright Idea.**
21. ——— **The Ghost in the Mill.**
22. ——— **Captain Kidd's Money.**
23. ——— **We and our Neighbours.** Double vol., 2s.
24. ——— **My Wife and I.** Double vol., 2s. ; cloth, gilt, 3s. 6d.
25. **Hans Brinker ; or, the Silver Skates.**
26. **Lowell's My Study Window.**
27. **Holmes (O. W.) The Guardian Angel.**
28. **Warner (C. D.) My Summer in a Garden.**
29. **Hitherto.** By the Author of "The Gayworthys." 2 vols., 1s. each.
30. **Helen's Babies.** By their Latest Victim.
31. **The Barton Experiment.** By the Author of "Helen's Babies."
32. **Dred.** By Mrs. BEECHER STOWE. Double vol., 2s. ; cloth, gilt, 3s. 6d.
33. **Warner (C. D.) In the Wilderness.**
34. **Six to One.** A Seaside Story.
35. **Nothing to Wear, and Two Millions.**
36. **Farm Ballads.** By WILL CARLETON.

Russell (W. Clarke). See "A Sailor's Sweetheart," 3 vols., 31s. 6d. ; "Wreck of the Grosvenor," 6s. ; "John Holdsworth (Chief Mate)," 6s.

Russell (W. H., LL.D.) The Tour of the Prince of Wales in India. By W. H. RUSSELL, LL.D. Fully Illustrated by SYDNEY P. HALL, M.A. Super-royal 8vo, cloth extra, gilt edges, 52s. 6d. ; Large Paper Edition, 84s.

SANCTA Christina: a Story of the First Century. By ELEANOR E. ORLEBAR. With a Preface by the Bishop of Winchester. Small post 8vo, cloth extra, 5s.

Seonee : Sporting in the Satpura Range of Central India, and in the Valley of the Nerbudda. By R. A. STERNDALE, F.R.G.S. 8vo, with numerous Illustrations, 21s.

Seven Years in South Africa : Travels, Researches, and Hunting Adventures between the Diamond-Fields and the Zambesi (1872—1879). By Dr. EMIL HOLUB. With over 100 Original Illustrations and 4 Maps. In 2 vols., demy 8vo, cloth extra, 42s.

Serpent Charmer (The): a Tale of the Indian Mutiny. By LOUIS ROUSSELET, Author of "India and its Native Princes." Numerous Illustrations. Crown 8vo, cloth extra, gilt edges, 7s. 6d.; plainer binding, 5s.

Shakespeare (The Boudoir). Edited by HENRY CUNDELL. Carefully bracketted for reading aloud; freed from all objectionable matter, and altogether free from notes. Price 2s. 6d. each volume, cloth extra, gilt edges. Contents:—Vol I., Cymbeline—Merchant of Venice. Each play separately, paper cover, 1s. Vol. II., As You Like It—King Lear—Much Ado about Nothing. Vol. III., Romeo and Juliet—Twelfth Night—King John. The latter six plays separately, paper cover, 9d.

Shakespeare Key (The). Forming a Companion to "The Complete Concordance to Shakespeare." By CHARLES and MARY COWDEN CLARKE. Demy 8vo, 800 pp., 21s.

Shooting: its Appliances, Practice, and Purpose. By JAMES DALZIEL DOUGALL, F.S.A., F.Z.A., Author of "Scottish Field Sports," &c. Crown 8vo, cloth extra, 10s. 6d.

"The book is admirable in every way..... We wish it every success."—*Globe.*
"A very complete treatise..... Likely to take high rank as an authority on shooting."—*Daily News.*

Silent Hour (The). See "Gentle Life Series."

Silver Pitchers. See ALCOTT.

Simon (Jules). See "Government of M. Thiers."

Six to One. A Seaside Story. 16mo, boards, 1s.

Smith (G.) Assyrian Explorations and Discoveries. By the late GEORGE SMITH. Illustrated by Photographs and Woodcuts. Demy 8vo, 6th Edition, 18s.

——— *The Chaldean Account of Genesis.* By the late G. SMITH, of the Department of Oriental Antiquities, British Museum. With many Illustrations. Demy 8vo, cloth extra, 6th Edition, 16s.

——— An entirely New Edition, completely revised and rewritten by the Rev. PROFESSOR SAYCE, Queen's College, Oxford. Demy 8vo, 18s.

Snow-Shoes and Canoes; or, the Adventures of a Fur-Hunter in the Hudson's Bay Territory. By W. H. G. KINGSTON. 2nd Edition. With numerous Illustrations. Square crown 8vo, cloth extra, gilt edges, 7s. 6d.; plainer binding, 5s.

Songs and Etchings in Shade and Sunshine. By J. E. G. Illustrated with 44 Etchings. Small 4to, cloth, gilt tops, 25*s.*

South African Campaign, 1879 *(The).* Compiled by J. P. MACKINNON (formerly 72nd Highlanders), and S. H. SHADBOLT; and dedicated, by permission, to Field-Marshal H.R.H. The Duke of Cambridge. 4to, handsomely bound in cloth extra, 2*l.* 10*s.*

South Kensington Museum. Published, with the sanction of the Science and Art Department, in Monthly Parts, each containing 8 Plates, price 1*s.* Volume I., containing 12 numbers, handsomely bound, 16*s.*

Stanley (H. M.) How I Found Livingstone. Crown 8vo, cloth extra, 7*s.* 6*d.*; large Paper Edition, 10*s.* 6*d.*

——— *"My Kalulu," Prince, King, and Slave.* A Story from Central Africa. Crown 8vo, about 430 pp., with numerous graphic Illustrations, after Original Designs by the Author. Cloth, 7*s.* 6*d.*

——— *Coomassie and Magdala.* A Story of Two British Campaigns in Africa. Demy 8vo, with Maps and Illustrations, 16*s.*

——— *Through the Dark Continent,* which see.

Story of a Mountain (The). By E. RECLUS. Translated by BERTHA NESS. 8vo, with Illustrations, cloth extra, gilt edges, 7*s.* 6*d.*

Story of a Soldier's Life (The); or, Peace, War, and Mutiny. By Lieut.-General JOHN ALEXANDER EWART, C.B., Aide-de-Camp to the Queen from 1859 to 1872. 2 vols., demy 8vo, with Illustrations.

Story of the Zulu Campaign (The). By Major ASHE (late King's Dragoon Guards), and Captain the Hon. E. V. WYATT-EDGELL (late 17th Lancers, killed at Ulundi). Dedicated by special permission to Her Imperial Highness the Empress Eugénie. 8vo, 16*s.*

Story without an End. From the German of Carové, by the late Mrs. SARAH T. AUSTIN. Crown 4to, with 15 Exquisite Drawings by E. V. B., printed in Colours in Fac-simile of the original Water Colours; and numerous other Illustrations. New Edition, 7*s.* 6*d.*

——— square 4to, with Illustrations by HARVEY. 2*s.* 6*d.*

Stowe (Mrs. Beecher) Dred. Cheap Edition, boards, 2*s.* Cloth, gilt edges, 3*s.* 6*d.*

Stowe (Mrs. Beecher) Footsteps of the Master. With Illustrations and red borders. Small post 8vo, cloth extra, 6s.

—— *Geography,* with 60 Illustrations. Square cloth, 4s. 6d.

—— *Little Foxes.* Cheap Edition, 1s.; Library Edition, 4s. 6d.

—— *Betty's Bright Idea.* 1s.

—— *My Wife and I; or, Harry Henderson's History.* Small post 8vo, cloth extra, 6s.*

—— *Minister's Wooing.* 5s.; Copyright Series, 1s. 6d.; cl., 2s.*

—— *Old Town Folk.* 6s.; Cheap Edition, 2s. 6d.

—— *Old Town Fireside Stories.* Cloth extra, 3s. 6d.

—— *Our Folks at Poganuc.* 10s. 6d.

—— *We and our Neighbours.* 1 vol., small post 8vo, 6s. Sequel to "My Wife and I."*

—— *Pink and White Tyranny.* Small post 8vo, 3s. 6d. Cheap Edition, 1s. 6d. and 2s.

—— *Queer Little People.* 1s.; cloth, 2s.

—— *Chimney Corner.* 1s.; cloth, 1s. 6d.

—— *The Pearl of Orr's Island.* Crown 8vo, 5s.*

—— *Little Pussey Willow.* Fcap., 2s.

—— *Woman in Sacred History.* Illustrated with 15 Chromo-lithographs and about 200 pages of Letterpress. Dem 4to, cloth extra, gilt edges, 25s.

Student's French Examiner. By F. JULIEN, Author of " Petites Leçons de Conversation et de Grammaire." Square crown 8vo, cloth, 2s

Studies in German Literature. By BAYARD TAYLOR. Edited by MARIE TAYLOR. With an Introduction by the Hon. GEORGE H. BOKER. 8vo, cloth extra, 10s. 6d.

* *See also* Rose Library.

Studies in the Theory of Descent. By Dr. AUG. WEISMANN, Professor in the University of Freiburg. Translated and edited by RAPHAEL MELDOLA, F.C.S., Secretary of the Entomological Society of London. Part I.—"On the Seasonal Dimorphism of Butterflies," containing Original Communications by Mr. W. H. EDWARDS, of Coalburgh. With two Coloured Plates. Price of Part. I. (to Subscribers for the whole work only), 8*s*; Part II. (6 coloured plates), 16*s*.; Part III., 6*s*.

Sugar Beet (The). Including a History of the Beet Sugar Industry in Europe, Varieties of the Sugar Beet, Examination, Soils, Tillage, Seeds and Sowing, Yield and Cost of Cultivation, Harvesting, Transportation, Conservation, Feeding Qualities of the Beet and of the Pulp, &c. By L. S. WARE. Illustrated. 8vo, cloth extra, 21*s*.

Sullivan (A. M., M.P.). See "New Ireland."

Sulphuric Acid (A Practical Treatise on the Manufacture of). By A. G. and C. G. LOCK, Consulting Chemical Engineers. With 77 Construction Plates, and other Illustrations. Royal 8vo, 2*l*. 12*s*. 6*d*.

Sumner (Hon. Charles). See Life and Letters.

Sunrise: A Story of These Times. By WILLIAM BLACK, Author of "A Daughter of Heth," &c. 3 vols., 31*s*. 6*d*.

Surgeon's Handbook on the Treatment of Wounded in War. By Dr. FRIEDRICH ESMARCH, Professor of Surgery in the University of Kiel, and Surgeon-General to the Prussian Army. Translated by H. H. CLUTTON, B.A. Cantab, F.R.C.S. Numerous Coloured Plates and Illustrations, 8vo, strongly bound in flexible leather, 1*l*. 8*s*.

Sylvan Spring. By FRANCIS GEORGE HEATH. Illustrated by 12 Coloured Plates, drawn by F. E. HULME, F.L.S., Artist and Author of "Familiar Wild Flowers;" by 16 full-page, and more than 100 other Wood Engravings. Large post 8vo, cloth, gilt edges, 12*s*. 6*d*.

TAUCHNITZ'S English Editions of German Authors. Each volume, cloth flexible, 2*s*.; or sewed, 1*s*. 6*d*. (Catalogues post free on application.)

——— *(B.) German and English Dictionary.* Cloth, 1*s*. 6*d*.; roan, 2*s*.

——— *French and English.* Paper, 1*s*. 6*d*.; cloth, 2*s*.; roan 2*s*. 6*d*.

Tauchnitz (B.) Italian and English Dictionary. Paper, 1s. 6d.; cloth, 2s. ; roan, 2s. 6d.

———— *Spanish and English.* Paper, 1s. 6d. ; cloth, 2s. ; roan, 2s. 6d.

———— *New Testament.* Cloth, 2s. ; gilt, 2s. 6d.

Taylor (Bayard). See "Studies in German Literature."

Through America ; or, Nine Months in the United States. By W. G. MARSHALL, M.A. With nearly 100 Woodcuts of Views of Utah country and the famous Yosemite Valley; The Giant Trees, New York, Niagara, San Francisco, &c.; containing a full account of Mormon Life, as noted by the Author during his visits to Salt Lake City in 1878 and 1879. In 1 vol., demy 8vo, 21s.

Through the Dark Continent : The Sources of the Nile; Around the Great Lakes, and down the Congo. By HENRY M. STANLEY. 2 vols., demy 8vo, containing 150 Full-page and other Illustrations, 2 Portraits of the Author, and 10 Maps, 42s. Seventh Thousand. Cheaper Edition, crown 8vo, with some of the Illustrations and Maps. 1 vol., 12s. 6d.

Tour of the Prince of Wales in India. See RUSSELL.

Trees and Ferns. By F. G. HEATH. Crown 8vo, cloth, gilt edges, with numerous Illustrations, 3s. 6d.

Two Friends. By LUCIEN BIART, Author of "Adventures of a Young Naturalist," "My Rambles in the New World," &c. Small post 8vo, numerous Illustrations, gilt edges, 7s. 6d. ; plainer binding, 5s.

Two Supercargoes (The) ; or, Adventures in Savage Africa. By W. H. G. KINGSTON. Numerous Full-page Illustrations. Square imperial 16mo, cloth extra, gilt edges, 7s. 6d. ; plainer binding, 5s.

UNDER the Punkah. By PHIL ROBINSON, Author of "In my Indian Garden." Crown 8vo, limp cloth, uniform with the above, 3s. 6d.

Up and Down ; or, Fifty Years' Experiences in Australia, California, New Zealand, India, China, and the South Pacific. Being the Life History of Capt. W. J. BARRY. Written by Himself. With several Illustrations. Crown 8vo, cloth extra, 8s. 6d.

BOOKS BY JULES VERNE.

WORKS.	Large Crown 8vo — Containing 350 to 600 pp. and from 50 to 100 full-page illustrations.		Containing the whole of the text with some illustrations.	
	In very handsome cloth binding, gilt edges.	In plainer binding, plain edges.	In cloth binding, gilt edges, smaller type.	Coloured Boards.
	s. d.	s. d.	s. d.	
Twenty Thousand Leagues under the Sea. Part I. Ditto. Part II.	10 6	5 0	3 6	2 vols., 1s. each.
Hector Servadac	10 6	5 0		
The Fur Country	10 6	5 0	3 6	2 vols., 1s. each.
From the Earth to the Moon and a Trip round it	10 6	5 0	2 vols., 2s. each.	2 vols., 1s. each.
Michael Strogoff, the Courier of the Czar	10 6	5 0		
Dick Sands, the Boy Captain	10 6	5 0		s. d.
Five Weeks in a Balloon	7 6	3 6	2 0	1 0
Adventures of Three Englishmen and Three Russians	7 6	3 6	2 0	1 0
Around the World in Eighty Days	7 6	3 6	2 0	1 0
A Floating City	7 6	3 6	2 0	1 0
The Blockade Runners			2 0	1 0
Dr. Ox's Experiment			2 0	
Master Zacharius	7 6	3 6	2 0	1 0
A Drama in the Air				
A Winter amid the Ice			2 0	1 0
The Survivors of the "Chancellor"	7 6	3 6	2 0	2 vols. 1s. each.
Martin Paz			2 0	1 0
THE MYSTERIOUS ISLAND, 3 vols.:—	22 6	10 6	6 0	3 0
Vol. I. Dropped from the Clouds	7 6	3 6	2 0	1 0
Vol. II. Abandoned	7 6	3 6	2 0	1 0
Vol. III. Secret of the Island	7 6	3 6	2 0	1 0
The Child of the Cavern	7 6	3 6		
The Begum's Fortune	7 6			
The Tribulations of a Chinaman	7 6			
THE STEAM HOUSE, 2 vols.:—				
Vol. I. The Demon of Cawnpore	7 6			
Vol. II. Tigers and Traitors	7 6			

CELEBRATED TRAVELS AND TRAVELLERS. 3 vols. Demy 8vo, 600 pp., upwards of 100 full-page illustrations, 12s. 6d.; gilt edges, 14s. each:—
   (1) THE EXPLORATION OF THE WORLD.
   (2) THE GREAT NAVIGATORS OF THE EIGHTEENTH CENTURY.
   (3) THE GREAT EXPLORERS OF THE NINETEENTH CENTURY.

WALLER (*Rev. C. H.*) *The Names on the Gates of Pearl*, and other Studies. By the Rev. C. H. WALLER, M.A. Second Edition. Crown 8vo, cloth extra, 6s.

—— *A Grammar and Analytical Vocabulary of the Words in* the Greek Testament. Compiled from Brüder's Concordance. For the use of Divinity Students and Greek Testament Classes. By the Rev. C. H. WALLER, M.A. Part I., The Grammar. Small post 8vo, cloth, 2s. 6d. Part II. The Vocabulary, 2s. 6d.

—— *Adoption and the Covenant.* Some Thoughts on Confirmation. Super-royal 16mo, cloth limp, 2s. 6d.

Warner (*C. D.*) *My Summer in a Garden.* Rose Library, 1s.

—— *Back-log Studies.* Boards, 1s. 6d.; cloth, 2s.

—— *In the Wilderness.* Rose Library, 1s.

—— *Mummies and Moslems.* 8vo, cloth, 12s.

Weaving. See " History and Principles."

Wills, A Few Hints on Proving, without Professional Assistance. By a PROBATE COURT OFFICIAL. 5th Edition, revised with Forms of Wills, Residuary Accounts, &c. Fcap. 8vo, cloth limp, 1s.

With Axe and Rifle on the Western Prairies. By W. H. G. KINGSTON. With numerous Illustrations, square crown 8vo, cloth extra, gilt edges, 7s. 6d.; plainer binding, 5s.

Woolsey (*C. D., LL.D.*) *Introduction to the Study of International Law*; designed as an Aid in Teaching and in Historical Studies. 5th Edition, demy 8vo, 18s.

Words of Wellington: Maxims and Opinions, Sentences and Reflections of the Great Duke, gathered from his Despatches, Letters, and Speeches (Bayard Series). 2s. 6d.

Wreck of the Grosvenor. By W. CLARK RUSSELL, Author of " John Holdsworth, Chief Mate," " A Sailor's Swee'heart," &c. 6s. Third and Cheaper Edition.

www.ingramcontent.com/pod-product-compliance
Lightning Source LLC
Chambersburg PA
CBHW031940230426
43672CB00010B/1988